Star Wars in Canadian Sociology

Star Wars in Canadian Sociology

Exploring the Social Construction of Knowledge

David A. Nock

Fernwood Publishing
Halifax

Chapter four was originally printed in *Society/Société* Vol. 12.3 (1988) as "John Porter: The Unknown Functionalist" and is reprinted here with permission of the Canadian Sociology & Anthropology Association. Chapter five was originally printed in *Fragile Truths: 25 Years of Sociology and Anthropology in Canada* and is reproduced here with permission of the Carelton University Press.

Editing: Anne Webb
Design and layout: Brenda Conroy
Printed and bound in Canada.
A publication of Fernwood Publishing.

Fernwood Publishing
Box 9409, Station A
Halifax, Nova Scotia
B3K 5S3

Canadian Cataloguing in Publication Data

Nock, David, 1949-
      Star Wars in Canadian Sociology
      Includes bibliographical references.
      ISBN 1-895686-18-0

1. Sociology -- Canada -- History.   I. Title.
HM22.C3N6 1993   301'.0971   C93-098531-1

This book is dedicated to Arthur Kent Davis,
who helped to launch my career in Sociology.

Contents

Acknowledgements

I would like to thank the Centre of Canadian Studies at the University of Edinburgh and its director, Ged Martin, as several of the chapters here were presented at or published in conferences or journals supported by the Centre—in particular, chapters two, three and six. Also I would thank Samuel D. Clark and the Department of Sociology at the University of Western Ontario, where I worked on chapters one, five and six. Chapter five, in fact, was first presented in a departmental seminar there. Being close to Richard Helmes-Hayes at the University of Waterloo was also a boon. The Canadian Sociology and Anthropology Association assisted in providing a forum for presenting several of the chapters. Chapters four and five were presented at sessions organized by Harvey Rich and Ed Silva and chapter two was read for me in my absence by Lakehead colleague Randle W. Nelson, who has also served as an able promoter of my work. Other colleagues who encouraged this work include the Strangers through whom I first met the likes of Michel Foucault and Hayden White, and David Peerla, a Stranger-in-absentia. I must also thank my university for granting me a sabbatical in the year 1989-1990, which resulted in this book. And thanks to Mary for making arrangements to come to London.

I would also like to note the work and support at Fernwood. Errol Sharpe I have always known as a friend of Canadian publishing and Canadian identity. Anne Webb helped to edit a difficult text. Brenda Conroy and Beverley Rach are also among the unseen assemblers and compilers. From my own department I would thank Karen Woychyshyn and Eleanor Maunula for composing various drafts of the manuscript.

Chapters two, four and five have been published in previous form, sometimes rather differently. These include " 'Crushing the Power of Finance': The Socialist Prairie Roots of S.D. Clark" *British Journal of Canadian Studies*, 1986, vol. 1, no. 1; "John Porter: The Unknown Functionalist" *Society/Société*, 1988, vol. 12, no. 3; and "Star Wars: The Social Construction of Reputation in Anglo-Canadian Society" in *Fragile Truths: 25 Years of Canadian Sociology and Anthropology in Anglo-Canadian Sociology*, 1992, eds. W.K. Carroll, L. Christiansen-Ruffman, R.F. Currie, and D. Harrison. Ottawa: Carelton University Press.

Introduction

In the last thirty years or so, there has been a type of revolution in views about epistemology—the study of how we know what we think we know. This revolution was marked by the publication of Thomas Kuhn's *The Structure of Scientific Revolutions* in 1962. Phrases such as "post-Kuhnian epistemology" now roll off the tongues of scholars. As with a lot of important books, its reception had as much to do with the times and the spirit of the age as with the book itself.

Older epistemologies had stressed the pursuit of a sort of "final" knowledge—an "objective" knowledge uninfluenced by concerns from the world outside of science, and rendered more precise by better methods. Kuhn emphasized that science even a highly mathematical science such as astronomy, was influenced by so-called external influences from the social world. Thus, for example, he pointed out in his earlier work, *The Copernican Revolution* (1957), how the fashionable status of astronomers as astrologers discouraged the early adoption of the Copernican view of the universe. In addition, the Church (which looked with disfavour upon astrology because of its apparent rejection of free will) rejected Copernicus' views for its own reasons. Kuhn also emphasized that scientific progress was often made on the basis of incomplete evidence, only partially supported beliefs, and even on the basis of faith, bias and self-interest.

Since then various theories have followed which have emphasized these points of externality and irrationality or arationality a good deal more than Kuhn would have desired. He maintained his faith in the process and logic of science, howevermuch the norms were broken in periods of paradigm revolution and breakdown. Modern critics influenced by Kuhn's own early source, Ludwik Fleck, have stressed that no form of knowledge is exempt from wider social influences, not natural science nor social science.

However, much of this epistemological revolution has been on the basis of abstract philosophical reasoning or somewhat remote historical case studies. When it comes to a particular subject such as sociology, a rather unreflective positivism or objectivism still seems in effect. Even when sociologists are aware of "post-Kuhnian epistemology" their work as sociologists generally seems divorced from its implications.

My aim in this book is to introduce certain epistemological perspectives in a readable fashion and then to apply the insights of post-Kuhnian epistemology to certain case studies in Canadian sociology.

Thus, in the case of S.D. Clark, John Porter, Robert Stebbins, Robert Brym and Bonnie Fox, and even myself, I have tried to show how external and non-rational factors affected the choice of the issue focused on and the nature of the analysis itself. I use the term non-rational here simply to mean that certain paths of analysis were followed for reasons partly not emanating directly from the socio-historical issue at hand.

It is not my belief that assumptions influenced by non-rational factors can be avoided, or that by making these assumptions one is engaging in "bad science." Once at a public presentation at a major university dealing with one of the case studies that follows, I heard some comments that suggested this. It seems that we as sociologists and as scientists want to believe otherwise. We want to believe that pristine, objective, final knowledge can be achieved. Others may fall into the trap of allowing extra-scientific factors to affect their work, but surely not ourselves!

In order to draw the reader to a different conclusion, I have focused on the work of some of the best and most eminent sociologists in Canada. I also devote a chapter to my own work to show how even it can be analyzed from a post-Kuhnian position. If I have done so successfully, I hope the reader will not reject my substantive work on the missionary E.F. Wilson as "exploded," but will see Wilson's contribution as all the more rich in meaning and implication.

The aim of this book is not to lull the reader into a relativistic torpor nor to come to the conclusion that pursuit of knowledge is a waste of time. Rather, it is to demonstrate that all reading and writing is hermeneutic (i.e. needs to be interpreted) and thus must be seen in light of the aphorism "there's more to this than meets the eye." Narratives of "fact" are always based on interpretation and, if we are not to fall into naive readings of texts, we must be aware of the general epochal influences on a writer and on ourselves as readers, and our own (and the author's) personal social location.

Addressing poststructuralism and postmodernism specifically (and relying upon post-Kuhnian epistemology more broadly), Ben Agger writes that such analyses "reject the possibility of presuppositionless representation, instead arguing that every knowledge is contextualized by its historical and cultural nature" (1991; 117). From this vantage point, reading must be a "strong activity, not merely passive reflection of an objective text with singular meaning" (ibid., 113). Perhaps the broadest goal of this book is to encourage readers of subjects such as sociology to react to texts rather than passively responding to the words on the page. Questions about who the author is, what his or her relationship is to the text, and the implications of the exact date of composition must always present themselves to the reader in the quest for meaning. (One factor among many is the use of gender-exclusive language in texts from earlier periods—and sometimes in current texts as well—as evident in material quoted in the following chapters.) The reader must also reflect on the social influences which might affect their own interpretation of a text.

Chapter One

The Positivist View of Science

In the history of sociology, as in society generally, the 1960s marked a watershed. Positivistic beliefs about the nature of science and social science which had previously met little critique were extensively challenged both by a renewed tradition in the sociology of knowledge and by the French and European modes of thought identified as post-modernism and poststructuralism. However, positivist-inspired research continues to be conducted; its characteristic beliefs and practices accord much better with utilitarian university and government studies interested in proving the usefulness of funded research than with traditions which assert that all observation and analysis is perspectival.

Positivism may be identified as the view that scientific observation is free of the contaminating conceptions, values, beliefs and ideologies of the scientific observer. The observer and the observed are two entirely separate and disconnected entities. What is attained is an "objective" understanding of the nature of the object being studied. At the bottom of this notion of science is the worship of "facts," defined as correctly observed and described data which are uncontaminated by the presuppositions of the scientist-observer. Werner Pelz suggests that positivism "wishes to 'let facts speak for themselves,' and recognizes no discourse as scientific, even as rational, beyond the language of facts, beyond that which can be factually verified" (1974; 71).

Such a view of the scientific enterprise presumes perception and conception can be clearly distinguished from each other. The scientist must be able to identify if and when conception interferes with perception. Good scientific work requires that a scientist hold a rather detached view of what is being observed so that emotions and prejudgments do not affect the observations made and the collection of facts. One way to control observation is to use sophisticated methods and methodologies, particularly those which include the use of statistics and mathematical language. Observations in this format are considered to be much better because they do not use languages that are culture-specific. When using other than scientific languages it is very difficult to render observations which are free of cultural influences. The stereotype of a positivistic scientist would probably depict someone in a white lab coat operating much highly elaborate machinery which arrived at observations using mathematics.

This conception of science is summed up clearly by Gwynn Nettler, Professor Emeritus at the University of Alberta: "Scientific explanations depend, then, upon facts" (1970; 94). Facts, according to Nettler, are real in that they reflect the external reality outside the scientific observer. It follows that scientific theories are invented "for the ordering of facts" (ibid., 95). Because a fact is a real representation of the external world, it "won't 'go away' just because one doesn't believe in it" (ibid., 94). This emphasis on facts helps distinguish scientific explanation from other forms. "While other explainways may use facts, they do not depend upon them" (ibid.).

The definition of "fact" as objective observation of reality is acclaimed by this conception. Nettler's view that "perception is *not* determined by conception" (ibid., 93), that perception and conception are separate, discrete activities is fundamental to a positivistic view of science. As one of the characteristics of science is objectivity, efforts must be made "to control personal and cultural bias in inference and observation" (ibid., 99) and to formulate scientific propositions such that they can be falsified by the finding of facts which may disprove theories. Positivistic thinkers such as Nettler are aware that conception may affect perception. He warns that inaccuracy in observation of fact is likely to result from "the impact of desire and other preconceptions upon perception" (ibid.). Besides training the scientist in "disinterestedness," Nettler advocates the development of "instruments and observational procedures that reduce the errors characteristic of simple experience" (ibid.).

Such a view of the scientist has, like everything else, evolved over time. It did not become mandatory to view scientists in this way until the last quarter of the eighteenth century. Wolf Lepenies uses Georges-Louis Buffon, an eighteenth century French scientist and author, to describe a scientific career before modern positivistic views of science became fixed. Buffon was a popularizer who, instead of emphasizing mathematics and method, wrote clear prose and used a minimum of statistics. After his election to the prestigious Academie Française in 1753, Buffon spoke on the subject of style. "The fact surprised no one: it was considered quite natural that a scientist should also regard himself as an author, as someone, that is, who paid heed not only to what he said but also to the way in which he said it, and who wished not only to instruct his public but also to entertain them as he did so" (Lepenies 1988, 3). Nevertheless, Buffon outlived his time and became "the first scholar to lose his reputation because he had devoted himself to author-ship and too little to research" (ibid.).

Positivist sociology developed somewhat later than positivist science. The word "sociology" was coined in the 1830s by Auguste Comte, but it remained a rather inconsequential subject until it became established in universities in the United States, France and Germany in the 1890s. Much debate ensued over whether sociology could exist and, if so, on what basis. In contrast to the natural sciences where, for the most part, the observer and the object of study are personally disconnected, in the study of society the observers belong in one way or another to a wide array of social institutions and do *not* belong to others. This situation led Wolf Lepenies to observe that sociology "had oscillated between a scientific orientation which has led it to ape the natural sciences and a hermeneutic attitude which has shifted the discipline towards the realm of literature" (1988, 1).

Efforts by the founders of sociology to validate the discipline by claiming it as a natural science were understandable as the natural sciences already enjoyed great prestige by the late nineteenth century.

The "Columbia School" of Positivistic Sociology

The school of Franklin H. Giddings, associated with Columbia University, was the most determined among the early sociologists in its drawing upon the prestige of natural science and positivism to justify the budding and not very secure "science of society." Giddings, who lived from 1855 to 1929, was most influential in producing a scientific positivist sociology during the last two decades of his life. An able group of graduate students went on to found a number of important departments such as Minnesota and North Carolina. In addition, the journal *Social Forces*, launched in 1922, became the house organ for this conception of sociology, edited as it was by a Giddings PhD student, Howard Odum.

In 1909, L.L. Bernard (not a Columbia-Giddings PhD, but one who was in sympathy with notions of a positivist sociology) compiled a fascinating report on "The Teaching of Sociology in the United States." This article contained comments from many sociologists about questions or issues that vexed them. Giddings' response to the qualitative concerns raised was typical in that he sought out men (sic) "not afraid to work; who will get busy with the adding machine and the logarithms, and give us *exact studies*, such as we get from psychological laboratories, not to speak of the biological and physical labs. *Sociology can be made an exact quantitative science*, if we get *industrious* men interested in it" (Bernard, 1909, 196). Despite this ringing proclamation for a mathematical sociology, Giddings and his own PhD students were initially less likely to use their adding machines than might be supposed, although it should be pointed out that Woofter, one of his students, did pioneer the use of the coefficient of correlation in a sociology doctoral dissertation (Bannister 1987, 86). Nevertheless, such a manifesto did distinguish Columbia from Chicago where the doing of sociology often meant field-work and participant observation rather than use of adding machines.

In 1927 Read Bain, a convert to Giddings-style sociology, compared Columbia sociology and Chicago sociology by contrasting the Chicago-controlled *American Journal of Sociology* with the Columbia-North Carolina-controlled *Social Forces*. He suggested that *Social Forces* paid "much more attention" to methods of investigation than the *AJS* (1927, 422), that the former had a "much greater number of illustrations, graphs, and tables than are found" in the *AJS* (ibid., 418) and that "the average length of the articles in *Social Forces* was 4.87 pages as against 19 pages in the *American Journal of Sociology*" (ibid.). The implication was that *Social Forces* read more like a series of natural science research reports, and the *AJS* like a series of literary essays.

Social Forces ran a continuous series of articles upholding Columbia-Giddings sociology. Giddings himself published articles that stressed that the work of sociology was measurement and the establishment of facts. In the early twenties he stated that "a true and complete description of anything must include measurements of it" (1922, 1), that "the *scrutiny* of alleged facts to determine whether or not they *are* facts, is the fundamental *systematic* work of science," and that this work involved "much repeating of observations and measurements" (1923, 509 and 513). Provocative articles were also written by Giddings' followers. George A. Lundberg, in his "Case Work and the Statistical Method" (case work being associated with Chicago sociology), stated that "the case method is not in itself a scientific method at all . . . the statistical method is the best, if not the only, scientific method of classifying and summarizing large numbers of cases" (1926-27, 61). Lundberg was a product of Stuart Chapin at Minnesota, who was in turn a student of Giddings.

Such attacks naturally drew responses from Chicago sociologists. Charles Ellwood, for example, did not deny that science is inductive in that it goes from "the facts" to "theories," but he differed when it came to the Giddings group's assumption that statistics comprise a privileged form of knowledge. He asserted that there could be several orders of facts besides the statistical, including the historical and the comparative-anthropological. The development of statistics as yet was "very small." Ellwood argued that a statistical method has still to "be enormously developed before it is susceptible of application to the more general problems of social behaviour. For this reason but little use can be made of the statistical method at the present time in dealing with the more general problems of sociology" (1923-24, 330).

A more frontal assault on Giddings' method appeared in the *AJS* in 1931. It was written by Herbert Blumer, a disciple of Robert Park, who was later to pioneer "symbolic interactionism," a mode of analysis in sociology which emphatically does not rely on adding machines. Blumer wrote that,

> few things are more irritating than to read a piece of research conforming most stringently to accredited techniques, abounding in numbers, or units, or elements, only to discover outstanding sloppiness in conceptual usage. Others may be impressed by the proficiency in the use of technique, or by the clean-cut numerical relations between units, but I only regret our stereotyped methodological notions which permit and encourage students to play with mental toys in the belief that the manipulation of these empty terms constitute science (1931, 533).

The Chicago School: Ambiguous Scientism

Despite its rejection of statistics as a privileged method in sociology, the Chicago School (in particular, that centred on Robert E. Park from 1915 to 1935) insisted that sociology must progress as a science. A key text in this regard was a joint effort of Park and his younger associate, E.C. Burgess. *Introduction to the Science of Society* (1970), an introductory textbook, ambitiously bore the name of science in its title in a way which most modern sociology textbooks would not. This textbook was somewhat advanced compared to most competitive textbooks. As Janowitz points out, there was "no conscious effort at popularization" (1970, xiii). Nevertheless "the green bible," as it came to be known, was regarded as the epitome of Chicago sociology and was the most used sociology textbook from 1921 to 1943.

The textbook begins with a discussion of Auguste Comte's program to extend to the social sciences "the positive methods of the natural sciences" (Park and Burgess 1970, 1). Substantial emphasis is placed by the authors on distinguishing history and sociology. History, they claim, is always concerned with date and location and with individual and particular circumstances. Because of this, "historical facts . . . cannot therefore be repeated, they are not subject to experiment and verification . . . a fact not subject to verification is not a fact for natural science" (ibid., 6). Natural science, in comparison, is concerned "not with individuals, but with classes, types, species." By "class" Park and Burgess mean "category" or a group of related phenomena. Relying on the German philosopher Windelband (whom Park studied under in Germany during the 1890s), they concur that natural science "seeks to formulate laws [history] to portray events. . . . The natural scientist considers the single case only so far as he can see in it the features which serve to throw light upon a general law" (ibid., 8). Sociology is seen as a natural science because rather than being interested in single historical events or situations, it seeks to produce generalizations or "laws" which are constant. "History . . . seeks to reproduce and interpret concrete events as they actually occurred in time and space. Sociology, on the other hand, seeks to arrive at natural laws and generalizations in regard to human nature, irrespective of time and place" (ibid., 11).

One of the key concepts in Parks' view of a scientific sociology was that of "natural history." This was the view that analogous social situations were comparable and thus could be conceptualized as a series of "typical events" which would confront the individual. A further illustration of Park's reliance on natural science was his development of "human ecology" as a theoretical paradigm. This involved adapting a paradigm applied to patterns of plant competition of interdependence to the study of human societies (Shore 1987, 98-101). In a book purporting to study human society, students were introduced to reprinted selections by natural scientists such as Charles Darwin and Frederick Clements (one of the pioneers of plant ecology). Some observers have felt that the human mind exalted the human species to such a degree that comparison to other animal and plant species was fruitless, but Park compared human interactions with those of both plants and animals.

Thus Park saw himself as a scientist. Like the positivists, he wanted the observer not to interact with the subject of study. He rejected sociologists both as activists and as social work-oriented do-gooders. Matthews writes that "Park himself had no doubt that a certain Olympian detachment was part of the essential make-up of a successful sociologist" (1977, 116). He told a group of students who wished to be activists for civil rights that they should investigate race relations with "the same objectivity and detachment with which the zoologist dissects the potato bug" (ibid.).

But despite some agreements with Giddings and the Columbia school, considerable differences remained. As noted above, Giddings saw statistics and adding machines as the privileged tools of sociology. Park did not. In his younger years, Park had gained considerable experience as a journalist (Matthews 1977, 8-11). He was on the city beat in Chicago and saw all the subcultures that were far removed from conventional citizens. As Matthews puts it, the reporter was "an institutionalized voyeur . . . . The city beat reporter from the first fulfilled the role of informal and intuitive sociologists, acting as eyes, ears, and moral censor for the audience . . . . " (ibid, 10). When Park came to the University of Chicago he emphasized direct observation and personal knowledge of city areas and subcultures over and above the collection of statistics or reliance on official records. Park's aim regarding method was to turn budding sociologists into "reporters-in-depth" (ibid., 108). Sometimes students were "treated to field trips, strolls through Chicago on which Park mused about the significance of what they saw" (ibid., 107).

Such a method fit into Park's own background and his sociological perspective. He felt it was necessary to understand the viewpoint of individuals caught up in specific situations (Matthews 1977, 32-33). According to Park, the influence of "human ecology" as a sorting mechanism, resulted in like-minded individuals tending to live in particular regions of the city (their "natural areas"). Natural areas did not necessarily coincide with official zones, but existed because of the natural consequences of competition. Different natural areas were distinct not just in material-economic terms but also "in culture, subjective values and perceptions . . . codes of conduct," and the "set of roles and criteria for status" (ibid., 141). Thus the necessity for the sociologist-cum reporter and scientist to meet characteristic persons from the differing natural areas. Another technique used involved collecting autobiographical documents, or "life-histories" as they were called, which were then analyzed to understand the processes of natural history involved, that is, the series of typical events and steps or stages that led to the present.

The emphasis on qualitative methodologies among analysts at Chicago reached a point where several British authors (Harvey 1987; Bulmer 1984) felt it necessary to try to balance it by emphasizing quantitative research at Chicago as well. Unlike the Giddings "school" which saw statistics as the "royal road" to scientific knowledge, Chicago sociologists were interested in many methods. Park himself seems to have had more than fragmentary doubts about statistics in sociology and appears to have resented the appointment of W.F. Ogburn to the Chicago faculty in 1927— the appointment aimed to rectify the lack of statistical sociology evident among the faculty. In an entry in Ogburn's journal he recounts being snubbed on arrival by Park who failed to invite him and his wife to a faculty party. "Next I was told repeatedly by various persons that Park spent a good deal of time in his classes belittling statistics and pointing out their limitation" (Harvey 1987, 20).

Thus the attitude of Robert Park and the Chicago School to an objectivistic scientific account of sociology was just a little ambivalent. Certainly Park and his colleagues saw themselves as scientists and quoted Charles Darwin and plant ecologists to prove it, but they did not quote the positivists' view on statistics. They were interested in process, in interactions in pre-existing social situations and the response of specific individuals, and particularly in typical sequences of responses that might add up to "laws" of human behaviour. Park and his associates wished to eschew sociological radicalism (Park himself apparently voted the Republican ticket all his life) and forms of sociology that wished to co-exist with social welfare. For this he has been trenchantly criticized recently by Mary Jo Deegan (1989) as this approach meant demeaning or ignoring a social activist sociology that was associated with prominent women.

Mannheim: Raising the Spectre of Relativism

Karl Mannheim (1893-1947) is often credited with "inventing" the sociology of knowledge in Germany during the 1920s and 1930s before his forced emigration to England after the rise of Hitler. Like most such claims, this one is excessive. German scholars had been toying with this idea for some years and a sociology of knowledge was at least implicit in the great founders of sociology. However, Mannheim's writing, in particular, *Ideology and Utopia* (1929, English edition 1936), did a great deal to expand the notoriety of the sociology of knowledge and its "principal thesis . . . that there are modes of thought which cannot be adequately understood as long as their social origins are obscured" (Mannheim 1936, 2).

Much of this popularity came from the topicality of Mannheim's book which deals with the social ideologies of the last several generations, including liberalism, conservatism, socialism, communism, and fascism. Mussolini was quoted extensively and, although Hitler had failed to make an impact by 1929, no doubt his rise added to the popularity of the English edition. Ideologies are those thought systems which are "used to stabilize a social order," while utopias are employed "when any transformation of that same order" (ibid., backcover) is attempted. Mannheim sought to demonstrate how such ideologies and utopias which pretend to be complete and objective representations of a greater truth are in fact socially conditioned. Marxism used a utopia to expose the class nature and ideological foundations of "bourgeois thought . . . and thereby to discredit it. Nowadays groups of every standpoint use this weapon against all the rest" (ibid. 1936, 75).

The word "ideology" has acquired a negative connotation in English (some aspects of the evaluation of this concept are traced by Mannheim), and tends to be associated with ideas which are obviously intended as propaganda. However, Mannheim demonstrated that much knowledge, even that taught in universities, is associated with specific ideologies. Traditional political economy, for example, was often critiqued by scholars (initially Marxist) for being tied to bourgeois perceptions and modes of thought. Mannheim was thus brought to the brink of relativism. This, in fact, is how he has been interpreted by some critics.

But Mannheim did establish a number of escape-hatches from relativism. Abercrombie points out that "one of the most consistent points in

[Mannheim's] work is the view that mathematical, logical and scientific beliefs are exempt from social causation; these beliefs form an autonomous realm . . . quite independent of social factors" (1980, 44-45). Even in reference to knowledge related to the social sciences his editor, Paul Kecskemeti, wrote that: "Mannheim's sociology of knowledge was often misunderstood as a variant of scepticism and illusionism. I shall try to show that his purpose was not to demonstrate the inescapability of relativism and scepticism, but rather the thesis that in spite of the inescapability of certain relativist conclusions, genuine knowledge of historical and social phenomenon was possible" (1959, 1).

An important element in this thesis was the distinction that Mannheim drew between *relativism* and *relationism*. Gregory Baum defines the former as "the approach that recognizes that all knowledge is socially dependent, bound to the location of the thinker, and reasons from this to the inevitable relativity of all human truth. Relationism, on the other hand, is the approach that also acknowledges the social dependency of knowledge but refuses to use this principle reductively as an argument for the relativity of all truth" (1977, 36). As Peter Novick puts it, Mannheim was "attempting to *escape* relativism" (1988, 159). He offered "three doors" through which one could move toward "at least a greater degree of objectivity" (ibid.). The first "door" comprised the approach that "the very awareness of the problem was part of the solution" (ibid.). The second "door" was the assertion that "though all knowledge was perspectival, the multiplication of perspectives, and their attempted reconciliation, could move one closer to objectivity" (ibid., 160). The third "door" was accessed by depending on the analyses of a socially detached "free-floating intelligentsia" which was not tied to specific social influences.

Each of these three "doors" caused much debate. Writing about the first "door" a prominent historian, Carl Becker, remarked: "Having relentlessly pressed all our heads down below the surface of the flowing social process, [Mannheim] first assures us that we can never get out, and then tells us that we can after all escape drowning by frankly recognizing that we are under water" (1988, 159). As far as the second "door" was concerned, Becker felt there was no reason why an enlarged "view of the whole" should not itself be "conditioned by the social situation in precisely the same way that the 'original standpoints' are" (ibid., 160). The third "door" was also attacked; many have pointed out the weakness of an argument that claims there is a "privileged" class which lives freer of social connections than other groups. This conception seems to assume an old-fashioned view of the "ivory-tower," but universities today are more the abode of business-oriented grant-seeking men and women than sheltered eccentrics.

The debate on objectivity seems to have been resolved less by the cogency of Mannheim's solutions than by a changing socio-economic environment. Novick has stressed that "the aftermath of World War I ushered in a period of negativity and doubt, the climate in which the relativist critique flourished" (1988, 281). It was in the Weimar Germany of the 1920s, with its incredibly variegated political and ideological *kampf*—that Mannheim's sociology of knowledge flourished. With the coming of the Second World War, the fascination with the problems posed by relativism faded. A war is a time for certainty and the dispelling of doubt, not for epistemological quibbles. As far as the sociologies of knowledge and science are concerned, Mannheim's legacy was an emphasis on "the epistemological distinction between scientific and socio-historical knowledge" (Mulkay 1983, 16). This distinction would remain unaltered until the next decade of doubt, the 1960s, that at least in certain ways resembled the ideological anarchy of Weimar Germany.

Merton: The Social Context of the Organization of Science
During the period between the decline of the Chicago School in the late 1930s and early 1940s and the mid 1960s, structural functionalism (or more simply, functionalism) became the predominant theoretical orientation (or "paradigm" to anticipate the language of Thomas Kuhn) of North American sociology. The two dominant proponents of this perspective were Talcott Parsons at Harvard and Robert K. Merton, a faculty member at Columbia University who studied at Harvard in the 1930s. The key standpoint of functionalism was, generally, an emphasis on values as independent and causative influences in structuring a society. While functionalism did not deny that economic and material factors might affect society, it did suggest that particular values were *not* invariably associated with socio-economic formations.

To some degree, functionalism represented a response to Marxist explanations for the rise of industrial-capitalism. It depended upon Max Weber's sociology of religion which attributed the capacity or failure of capitalism to emerge in various world civilizations to the religious and social values which encouraged or impeded capitalism. Parsons had studied at Weber's place of work—the University of Heidelberg—in the 1920s after Weber's death, but while his influence was still felt. At this time Weber's influence on American sociology and social science was still minimal (Wells 1979); and it took the influence of Parsons himself to raise the image of Weberian sociology in the United States.

Merton's interest in the sociologies of knowledge and science lasted into the 1980s. His sociology of knowledge revealed rather clearly his Weberian-Parsonian functionalist roots. His doctoral dissertation on "Science, Technology and Society in Seventeenth Century England" (1938) pointed out the "unintended consequences of Puritanism on the motivation of early scientists" (Crothers 1987, 127). Merton had taken a line or so from Weber's writing and turned it into a thesis. He argued that religion, so often seen as the enemy of science, had acted as the seedbed of the scientific revolution in the seventeenth century. Moreover, it was from "the otherwise unlikely dour and theologically encumbered Puritan/Pietist sects that this impetus had specifically sprung" (ibid., 127).

By the late 1930s, Merton reacted to the "threatening loss of autonomy of German science in the Nazi era" (ibid.) by "attempting to analyse the cultural conditions which support scientific work" (ibid.). He underlined a number of norms integral to values taken as necessary for the pursuit of science. These norms included *universalism* (as opposed to ethnocentrism, racism and particularism), *communism* (to "denote the fact that there is common ownership of goods in the scientific community" [Sklair 1973, 112]), and a rejection of secrecy in the system of communication. He also advocated *disinterestedness*, inferring that scientists should put the goals of science above personal interests, and *organized scepticism*. This approach requires scientists to be interested above all in learning about the reality of the external, and thus be led by the factual quality of their observations. Given the tension-fraught period that these values emerged from, it was not surprising that they were seen to accord best with liberal democracies as opposed to the Nazi regime (Sklair 1973, 111). It is of interest to the sociology of knowledge to observe that Merton's norm of communism had to be redubbed "communalism" in the 1950s when communism as a political configuration lost its status as an ally during the Second World War and became identified as an enemy by the late 1940s (ibid., 112-113).

In the late 1960s and 1970s, this normative scheme of Merton's came under attack on empirical grounds; it was considered uncharacteristic of the way science truly operates (ibid., 118). Behind the actual empirical work undermining Merton's observations was an altered social climate. In the 1930s and 1940s liberal democracies were interpreted in a rather idealistic fashion as they opposed fascism, Nazism, and later Stalinist communism. Novick suggests that the rejection of relativism and espousal of positivism and objectivism had much to do with "the epistemological politics of the cold war" (1988, 297) and the Second World War: "The coming of World War II saw American culture turn toward affirmation and the search for certainty" (1988, 281). The Mertonian scheme suited this mood well, but by the 1960s and 1970s, with the discredited American presence in Vietnam, the revelation of anti-liberal anti-universalistic forces in American society such as white American resistance to racial equality and the collapse of politicians' credibility (during the Johnson-Nixon years), the mood turned against a celebration of the western system of power and its values. Merton's sociology of knowledge began to suffer.

Merton conducted or sponsored much other work on the organization of science, most of which was concerned with the stratification and hierarchy of the discipline. By and large Merton viewed these characteristics as inevitable but positive for the development of science as a whole, even if specific individuals were negatively affected. What Merton failed to address was the content of scientific work which was, as Mannheim had suggested, beyond ordinary discourse. He pointed out that external social contexts affected the functioning of science as did the internal organization of science, but he did *not* address the content of scientific knowledge. Novick suggests that this "scrupulous, almost phobic, avoidance of any sociologically informed discussion of the content of science" was "one of the most striking aspects of sociology of science before the 1960s . . . sociologists avoided content" (1988, 297). In part, this stemmed from Merton's own early (1938) conviction that "totalitarian theorists have adopted the radical relativistic doctrines . . . as a political expedient for discrediting 'liberal' or 'bourgeois' or 'non-Aryan' science" (quoted in Novick 1988, 289).

Thomas Kuhn and The Structure of Scientific Revolutions
The 1960s and 1970s brought an unprecedented challenge to positivistic ideas about science. This view of science, it should be remembered, depends on the notion that science is fact-driven, that "facts" are small items of empirical data observed by the subject about an external object, that science proceeds on the basis of disinterestedness and a lack of passion, and that scientists are ready to shed their conceptions rather quickly in light of disconfirming facts. In addition, it holds that truth is objective and final when in fact truth is found. The idea is that as a rule external nature does not change, but when it does the changes are predictable and can be "factored in."

The key text to upset this apple cart was by scientist-historian Thomas Kuhn. Peter Novick suggests Kuhn's 1962 text, *The Structure of Scientific Revolutions*, was "the vehicle which introduced the general academic world to what may be called, to be in fashion, 'postpositivist' or 'postempiricist' conceptions of science" (1988, 526). Although Kuhn was a natural scientist whose earlier work had dealt with the history of astronomy, his ideas became widely influential among scholars in very different fields. Novick suggests that it would be "hard to nominate another twentieth-century American work" (ibid., 526) which comes near to it in influence.

Kuhn talks about the reliance of scientists on paradigms. There has been considerable debate about what Kuhn means exactly by this term. In his own words, it refers to "models from which spring particular traditions of scientific research" (1970, 10). This notion of paradigm is paramount to Kuhn's conception of science—he suggests that scientists are socialized into accepting the prevailing paradigm prior to their scientific investigations. The "facts" that their investigations elicit are simply those facts which are called forth by the questions and expectations of the paradigm. What is not seen by the paradigm to be a legitimate concern is ignored. In the natural sciences only one paradigm is normally accepted in a particular field. This clearly distinguishes it from sociology where many paradigms prevail at one time. According to Kuhn, this is seen by scientists as wasteful and prescientific. Their image of the paradigm is that of a gigantic jigsaw puzzle with each scientist filling one small segment of the puzzle. To be working on several puzzles at the same time would be to waste resources and human capacity.

When scientists are socialized to adopt the dominant paradigm they typically are not taught alternatives or encouraged and equipped to make analytical judgements about the worth of rival paradigms (certainly a characteristic of sociology). They are taught to accept the paradigm as a "given." "Normal science" is the term Kuhn uses to refer to the "normal" situation in natural science where one paradigm predominates. In such a situation "No part of the aim of normal science is to call forth new sorts of phenomena . . . . Nor do scientists normally aim to invent new theories, and they are often intolerant of those invented by others" (Kuhn 1970, 24). Kuhn does not shrink from using the term "restricted vision" in reference to normal science, and states that its practitioners are normally engaged in "mopping-up operations . . . throughout their careers" (ibid.), not in marching out boldly to uncover new areas. Kuhn himself suggests that "the most striking feature" of normal researchers is "how little they aim to produce major novelties, conceptual or phenomenal" (ibid., 35).

As might be inferred from the above, shifting from one paradigm to another is not an easy or happy procedure in scientific research. Such epochs are extraordinary and cause discomfort. When anomalies are uncovered they may provoke a crisis, although the first reaction is to somehow "fit them" into the dominant paradigm. If the anomalies are sufficient, then a new paradigm may emerge, but the process which is necessary to replace the older paradigm is both political and religious in nature. It is appropriate to refer to such situations as scientific "revolutions." Kuhn refers to changing paradigms as "a conversion experience" (ibid., 151). Such conversion experiences are often difficult for older scientists since their "productive careers have committed them to an older tradition" (ibid.) and their personal prestige is tied up with the besieged paradigm. The facts necessary for the introduction of a new paradigm are never complete, therefore appealing to "facts" as a reason for paradigm change is never completely satisfactory. When a new candidate paradigm is proposed it has "seldom solved more than a few of the problems that confront it . . . it is only much later, after the new paradigm has been developed, accepted, and exploited that apparently decisive arguments . . . are developed" (ibid., 156).

Kuhn suggests that "personal and inarticulate aesthetic arguments" (ibid., 158) influence the selection of an alternative paradigm. He points out the importance of external and, in some cases, irrational influences in paradigm selection: "the sun worship that helped make Kepler a Copernican [lies] outside of science entirely" (ibid., 152-153).

Such observations reveal how far this conception of science is from the positivist view. Rather than being fact-driven, science is primarily paradigm-driven; disinterestedness is frequently breached, at least in times of extraordinary science; and scientists do not readily shed their views in response to facts, but are conservatives who attempt to ignore or incorporate anomalies.

The reception of *The Structure of Scientific Revolutions* was undeniably influenced by the spirit of the 1960s—iconoclastic and anti-authoritarian as it was. The early 1940s to the early 1960s, a period of "affirmation and consensus" which had been "congenial to an objectivist posture" (Novick 1988, 415), was over. "The sixties were years of distrust" (ibid.) and the "brazen mendacity" of the United States government led to a skepticism not just about "official truth," but "about truth of any kind—not least the academic" (ibid., 416). Even right-wing country poet Merle Haggard could write about seeing President Nixon lying "to us all on t.v." ("Are the Good Times Really Over").

The "Edinburgh School": Society and the Content of Science
With the altered social climate of the 1960s and the ascendancy of a very successful assault on traditional positivism (in the form of Thomas Kuhn) sociologists of knowledge began to cast doubt on previously accepted truths. A significant revision was effected by the so-called Edinburgh School which included Barry Barnes and David Bloor and was affiliated with the University of Edinburgh. Bloor observed that much of what had previously been published in the sociology of knowledge had been about science's "institutional framework and . . . factors relating to its rate of growth or direction" (Bloor 1976, 1). Earlier sociologists, such as Karl Mannheim, had left "untouched the nature of the knowledge thus created" (ibid.) out of the conviction that scientific knowledge was beyond social

influence. Bloor regarded such a stance as "a betrayal of their disciplinary viewpoint." He attributed the "hesitation to bring science within the scope of a thorough-going sociological scrutiny" to a "lack of nerve and will" (ibid., 2). The Edinburgh School began to narrow the gap traditional epistemology had asserted between science and ideology. Barry Barnes' warned that the reputation for "disinterest enjoyed by scientists may give spurious legitimation to values which are incorporated in their knowledge claims" and observed that "overt prescription is mingled with description in a great deal of bona fide science" (1974, 126). Henceforth analysis of scientific production would *not* proceed on the basis that science is a "privileged" path to knowledge. Instead, science came to be seen as "a part of culture like any other" (ibid., 99).

One issue that began to attract increasing attention in the new approach to the sociology of knowledge was the debate about "internal" and "external" factors in the history of science. The traditional view of scientific development, allied with positivistic and objectivistic ideas, held that science was a "self-contained activity, considered without reference to the surrounding material or cultural environment" (Novick 1988, 295), which "progressed" purely on the basis of logical and rational factors within the field itself. Because such a view was both self-flattering to scientists and useful for challenging totalitarian ideologies (which clearly and blatantly twisted the "truth"), "internalism" became "in the history of science not just a method, but a fighting faith" (ibid., 296).

The Edinburgh School began to push out the boundaries of the externalist argument. It has been recognized for decades, even if grudgingly, that scientific work is influenced by the amount and type of support it receives from the external society. After all, Merton's 1938 doctoral dissertation asserted an association between the rise of science and English puritanism (see Barnes 1974, 99, 104, 106 for references to this type of externalist discourse). The Edinburgh School went further, however, and applied externalist arguments to scientific *content*. For example, in 1971 Paul Forman sought to demonstrate a "link between philosophy and physics in the cultural context of the Weimar republic" in the 1920s (Barnes 1974, 109). At this time Heisenberg and Schrödinger developed quantum mechanics which was seen to be *acausal*, denying strict determinism and causation. The notion of acausality had been developing in philosophical circles in Germany, for example in the work of Oswald Spengler, since the turn of the century. As Barnes puts it, "The acausality of the scientists is derived from the acausality dominating the wider milieu; it occurs later than the latter, and as a response to it" (ibid., 110). In the same vein, Robert Young demonstrates that the work of Charles Darwin "cannot be seen as a technical controversy, turning on how well the available biological and geological materials fitted into the evolutionary framework" (ibid.). Young observes that Darwin "found" in nature "the same kind of division of labour at work as that found in the English factory system" and thus provided "a scientific guarantee of the rightness of the property and work relations of industrial society" (Rifkin 1984, 89).

It is interesting to note that Kuhn came to disapprove of the ways in which his work was being used, and he specifically mentioned Barnes (Kuhn 1977, xxi). He states: "My own work has been little concerned with the specification of scientific values, but it has from the start presupposed their existence and role" (ibid., xxi). Novick suggests that, "At no point did Kuhn ever abandon that orthodox 'internalist' posture which, as we have seen, dominated historiography of science in the postwar years" (1988, 533). Clearly this misrepresents Kuhn who, as already mentioned, considered "sun worship" an influence in Kepler's decision to support Copernicus' view of the sun and planets.

However, it is probably true that the Edinburgh School significantly extended Kuhn's ideas in ways he did not intend. Kuhn's ideas about external and irrational factors applied only to periods of scientific revolutions (extraordinary science) not to "normal science" when a dominant paradigm was securely in place. The Edinburgh School saw such factors as influencing science at all times. Science, in this view, was never exempt from outside cultural and social contexts.

Michel Foucault: Science as a Form of Power

The positivist and objectivist conception of science was not only under attack because of the influence of Thomas Kuhn and the Edinburgh School, but also because of a school of thought often referred to as postmodernism. This school attracted much attention in the 1960s in France, but since much of the work was not translated into English for several years, its impact did not reach its peak until the 1970s and 1980s in the English-speaking Western world. Initially the impact of postmodernism was felt in philosophy and departments of literature, then in history, and perhaps lastly in sociology. None of the prominent postmodernists was a sociologist and their writing was often far removed from the straightforward (perhaps too straightforward) prose of research-oriented sociologists. Since postmodernists stressed multiple meanings, irony, paradox and discontinuity, and since they did not emerge out of sociology, their delayed impact on the discipline is understandable.

The postmodernist who has had the greatest affect on sociology is Michel Foucault, perhaps because his interest in institutions and themes such as prisons, asylums, medicine and sexuality overlapped with those of sociologists (other postmodernists often analyzed literary or philosophical texts).

Understanding Foucault is easier when both his own history and that of French thought in the 1940s and 1950s are taken into consideration. Born in 1926, Foucault studied philosophy and was a communist until 1951. Up until the 1970s communism strongly appealed to French intellectuals.[1] In the 1950s Foucault studied psychology and spent much time in "observing psychiatric practice in mental hospitals" and teaching and publishing "material about psycho-pathology" (Sheridan 1980, 5). Foucault was thus working in a field in which the natural sciences and the social sciences intersect. He was interested from the beginning in "the political status of science and the ideological functions which it could serve" (Foucault 1980, 109). As a disillusioned communist, he was stimulated in this direction because of the Lysenko affair. Trofim Lysenko was a Soviet biologist who held outrageous and discredited ideas, but received the support of Joseph Stalin and the Soviet state.

Determined to study the intersection of science and "its relations with the political and economic structures of society" (ibid.), Foucault rejected the "harder" natural sciences on the grounds that proving their links to the social system would be to pose "an excessively complicated question" (ibid.). Rather, the "interweaving of effects of power and knowledge" could be grasped more easily "in the case of a science as 'dubious' as psychiatry" (ibid.). Later, when Foucault studies medicine more extensively in *The Birth of a Clinic* he observes it has a "much more solid scientific armature than psychiatry, but it too is profoundly enmeshed in social structures" (ibid.). From the beginning, then, Foucault stressed the links between science, society, power and knowledge. In so doing, he rejected and was rejected by the traditional positivistic stance of French communists. But, according to Foucault, "The price Marxists paid for their fidelity to the old positivism was a radical deafness to a whole series of questions posed by science" (ibid., 110).

If on the one hand Foucault rejected the positivism of the communists, he also rejected the reigning French philosophical fad of existentialism associated with Jean-Paul Sartre. Existentialism stresses "the individual subject's freedom of choice" in the world (Sheridan 1980, 4) and suggests that it is up to each individual to construct a meaning out of life. Foucault, along with a growing wave of structuralists, wished to "displace the human subject . . . from the centre of theoretical concern" (ibid., 90).

In his writing Foucault comes to concentrate on discontinuity and *epistemes*. or "systems of thought." Sheridan defines the term as "the underlying set of rules governing the production of discourses in any single period" (ibid., 209). Since postmodernists reject the idea of science having a privileged claim to knowledge, they adopted the word "discourse" to refer to any form of rational analysis.

Foucault's claims that *epistemes* are displaced from time to time and that little in the way of overlap is retained. One moves from one world of discourse to another with little cumulative development, although he notes that "the great biological image of a progressive maturation of science still underpins a good many historical analyses" (Foucault 1980, 112). Foucault points to medicine in which, in the eighteenth century, there appeared transformations which "broke not only with the 'true' propositions which it had hither to been possible to formulate but also, more profoundly; with the ways of speaking and seeing . . . . These are not simply new discoveries, there is a whole new 'regime' in discourse and forms of knowledge. And all this happens in the space of a few years" (ibid.).

Foucault's work has faced strong criticism from historians as he attacks what Mark Poster calls "the continuity thesis" (Poster 1984, 75) and seeks to "disrupt the easy, cozy intimacy that historians have traditionally enjoyed in the relationship of the past to the present" (ibid., 74). At a deeper level, Foucault challenges the appeal to reason, which historically undergirds most social science. He points out how, especially since the eighteenth century, reason as used by science has become "a form of power" (Poster 1984, 13).

Hayden White and the Collapse of the Narrative

Postmodernism has also cast doubt on the objectivity of traditional narrative accounts which are intended to show how a particular event results logically from prior events and situations. As John Murphy puts it, "For postmodernists, truth divorced from interpretation is fatuous. Accordingly, all knowledge is understood to be fully mediated by the human presence" and, "because the mind and reality are intertwined, truth does not have the autonomy to restrict thought" (Murphy 1988, 601). Compare such an approach with Columbia-Giddings student W.F. Ogburn's statement that "scientific verification restricts intellectual activities to the evidence and limits the mental associations that are dictated by emotion, which form such an attractive part of less restricted intellectual work" (1934, 215).

In the United States, history was confronted by Hayden White who assaulted "historians' most sacred boundary," that being the distinction between history and fiction or literature (Novick 1988, 600). In his 1973 *Metahistory: The Historical Imagination in Nineteenth-Century Europe* what interests White is not an analysis or re-examination of what various important historians have said about specific times or places and whether their accounts are still valid. Rather, he contends that all historical narratives are constructed according to an implicit plot. There are a range of alternative plotting structures which may be utilized by an author. Any narrative may depend upon one of four modes of emplotment, four modes of argument, and four modes of ideological implication (White 1973, 29). White suggests that "before the historian can bring to bear upon the data of the historical field the conceptual apparatus he will use to represent it, he must first *pre*figure the field—that is to say, constitute it an object of mental perception" (White 1973, 30). In other words, before an historian can write a narrative account, she or he explicitly or implicitly (but more usually the latter) must have selected the particular narrative structure into which the "facts" will fit. White infuriated traditional positivistic historians who saw themselves as historical Sergeant Fridays just "investigating the facts." For example, Novick critiques White's "trivializing of questions of evidence" (1988, 601) citing White's statement that "there are no grounds to be found in the record itself for preferring one way of construing its meaning rather than another" (ibid.).

John Murphy also focuses his sights on sociology asserting that postmodernists "remark that traditionally sociologists have had 'realist pretentions,' and thus the interpretive meaning of events has been regularly overlooked" (1988, 601). Instead of trying to "prove" definite conclusions about external reality, postmodernists are much more concerned with analyzing the techniques of language and concept use. They tend to take the narrative accounts of those who hold to "realist pretentions" and deconstruct them by identifying the modes of emplotment and language used to produce a certain effect. Seen in this manner, it is easy to criticize postmodernism for failing to contribute to our understanding of the external world; however, it can just as easily be defended for its capacity to deconstruct the "facts" upon which our understandings are based.

Conclusion
Departments of sociology have responded in various ways to what Novick refers to as "postpositivist" conceptions of science. No doubt most graduate students will encounter Thomas Kuhn's work at some point. It is much less likely that they will come across the Edinburgh School or postmodernism. As for undergraduates, many will not be introduced to any of the postpositivistic accounts of knowledge.

The reason for this, it would appear, is that there are some truths which are not palatable and which go against the grain of our mythologies. Additionally, social science still justifies itself to both citizens and government by contributing "reliable" data and for such a task the positivist conception of social science is the most effective. However, it may be argued that in order to understand key sociological writings in Canada "postpositivist" conceptions of knowledge must be utilized.

There is an old epistemological story worth telling here.[2] According to the story, three baseball umpires seek to explain their activity. "Some pitches are balls, and others are strikes and that's because they fit or not into the strike zone," says the first umpire. "I call the pitches balls or strikes depending on how I see them—it's a matter of my perception," says the second. "There are no such things as balls and strikes until I decide what they are," says the third umpire. The point is that our study of any subject involves *all three* approaches. There *is* some kind of external world out there which is independent of the observer; however, what we construct as forms of knowledge depends on how we see or perceive the world. The observer does not simply collect external facts, but is part of a "hermeneutic" or interpretive circle. Hermeneutics came into widespread use as it became evident that no reader of a document has a definitive reading. Rather, all readings are based on interpretations which, in turn, are based upon particular values and presuppositions. The error of scientific positivism and objectivism is its assumption that only the first umpire fits into what science actually is. Realistically the approaches of all three umpires must be taken any reading or observation of our society.

The following chapters are intended to act as case studies in the evolution from positivist to post-Kuhnian epistemology. If we take the positivist assumption we assume, or at least hope, that each study of the author is the final "definitive" word on its subject. We assume that each is written solely from a detached non-involved position by the author, and that essentially each author is simply observing facts of nature or facts of society as they are revealed by exact methodological instruments.

Following from post-Kuhnian epistemology, we assume that external and non-rational factors may influence the choice and treatment of each subject at hand. If such factors affected the timing and content (and resistance to) the Copernican Revolution, then surely we will find such factors in sociology. At the time of the Copernican revolution, the revival of neo-Platonist philosophy and mysticism in the Renaissance placed a premium on exact mathematics and upon the key role of the Sun as a geological representation of Divine Power. Such ideas plus a general milieu of change and flux in society more generally (such as the discovery of the New World, the Protestant Reformation, the Peasant Revolts) provided encouragement to Copernicus to foster his audacious theory (Kuhn 1957). Progress in science did not occur simply because of characteristics innate to science itself.

In the following chapters we see that S.D. Clark chose to emphasize the independence of frontier settlements from older centres of civilization in part because his background in the Alberta of the 1920s and 1930s with its own agrarian ferment resembled, or could be made to resemble, earlier struggles for frontier independence and liberation. As late as 1935, Alberta's Social Credit promised to free rural and small-business Albertans from the high costs of eastern-controlled finance.

In the case of John Porter, I show that his rather stereotyped analysis of the Anglican church in Canada has as much to do with his wider personal concern that Canada reject British values in favour of American values (closely linked in his own mind to a favourable nation of "modernity"). Thus the Anglican church of Canada is represented by him as simply an extension of the "Mother" country instead of as an adapting, evolving institution.

In the case of Brym and Fox and Stebbins, I show how regional factors affect citation practices rather than simply being (as positivists would have it) mirror representations of what is available in the field. We tend to cite people who are close to ourselves regionally, personally or theoretically and methodologically.

In the case of Chapter six, I illustrate how various author's images of the missionary figure of E.F. Wilson have varied according to the decade of each author and the particular social location of each. I also venture to discuss the motivations, both conscious and subconscious, which coalesced to produce my own biographical portrait.

Thus the following chapters assert that external and non-rational factors do affect how any scholar arrives at a particular analysis or narrative, and show how this operates concretely in actual sociological and historical production.

Notes

[1] The communist movement has traditionally held to a rigid positivistic and objectivistic view of scientific truth and felt that such an approach could be extended to the human or social sciences. Thus, for example, Thomas Kuhn was criticized by the communist left for his relativism (see Novick 1988, 422-23).

[2] This story was told by social philosopher Alex Michelos at the 1989 annual meeting of the Ontario Association of Sociology and Anthropology.

Chapter Two

'Crushing the Power of Finance': The Socialist Prairie Roots of S.D. Clark

The Changing Image of S.D. Clark

S.D. Clark played a pivotal role in the development of Canadian sociology. As one of the few academic sociologists in Canada before the expansion of the subject in the 1960s, he founded and was the first chair of the Department of Sociology at the University of Toronto. Prior to that he had been the main sociologist in the celebrated interdisciplinary Department of Political Economy at the same university. From 1939 onwards, while in this position, Clark wrote a series of works which commented on the nature of Canadian social development in the context of the Canadian staples and frontier economy, engaging what can be regarded as a type of macrosociology.

Clark's contributions have been acknowledged by both academic and government bodies. He became the president of the élite Royal Society of Canada in 1975, having previously been the president of its Humanities and Social Sciences section. He was awarded membership in the Order of Canada, was invited to be the editor of the Rockefeller series on the development of the Social Credit in Canada, and was made an Honorary Life Member of the Canadian Sociology and Anthropology Association. The only comparable figures in English Canadian sociology are Carl Dawson and John Porter (Wilcox-Magill 1983).

Yet Clark's is not controversial. His method of research is thoroughly historical in nature, and he became increasingly conservative at a time when Canadian sociology was becoming more and more materialist and even Marxist. Clark's work is often not read at all, is read superficially, or is misinterpreted because readers assume that what Clark came to represent in the 1960s and 1970s was the same or similar to what he had stood for in the 1930s, 1940s and 1950s when his scholarly reputation was first established. Clark did not alleviate this sort of misinterpretation when he published a number of works which seemed intended to discourage aspirants to the new materialist, neo-Marxist sociology now predominant in Canadian sociology (Clark 1979).

The assessment of Clark as a conservative is revealed in Dusky Lee Smith's comment that, "Some readers will have difficulty accepting the view that Clark was a young radical as well as in accepting the radical or critical nature of his [earlier] sociological form" (Smith 1983, 360). R. James Sacouman states that "S.D. Clark's works are a major example of the idealist perspective" (1983, 159), that Clark "consistently develops a non-Marxist classless theory" (ibid., 157), and that "his principles and focus of analysis are the antithesis to those of Marx" (ibid., 158).

No doubt the most ambitious presentation of this interpretation of Clark is provided by Deborah Harrison who devotes an entire book, *The Limits of Liberalism: The Making of Canadian Sociology,* plus a major article (1983) to the proposition that, "while ostensibly operating from a wholistic and historical conception of his society, Clark has nevertheless become trapped within the American functionalist assumption that sociology is fundamentally about individual behaviour and decision making. How, while being passionately preoccupied with his society, Clark has at the same time attempted to be a liberal individualist, in a country where one cannot do both" (1981, 16).

This dichotomy leads Harrison to outline two traditions of scholarship: the collective and the individualist. The former tradition includes such a mixed bag of Canadian scholars as Donald Creighton, Stanley Ryerson, Harold Innis, Mel Watkins, R.T. Naylor and Carl Cuneo, and is considered positive and progressive by Harrison; she feels the work of these scholars dwells on the survival of "the collective lives of groups and societies in terms of their abilities to survive over time" (1981, 14) rather than on "individuals on the make." For Harrison it is extremely important that Canadian scholarship identify with the collective tradition because of the precariousness of the Canadian state as it stands face to face with the American imperialist juggernaut. The individualist tradition which Harrison decries includes such scholars as F.J. Turner, Harry Johnson, Frank Underhill, Marcus Hansen, and the structural functionalist school of sociology in general, in addition to Clark himself. The impact of such an assessment is to dismiss Clark's work as essentially un-Canadian in its content, as pro-American in its individualistic orientations, and essentially as pro-imperialist and therefore unprogressive and un-Marxist. Such an interpretation by Harrison, Sacouman and Smith dismisses Clark as a figure in the progressive, materialist, neo-Marxist Canadian sociology movement and could remove him from his pedestal as a founder of Canadian sociology.

In the later part of his career, these characterizations of Clark begin to take on more validity. In 1953, in his mid-forties, Clark joined the establishment party in federal politics, the Liberal party of Canada, leaving behind him his former identification with the social democratic and quasi-socialist party, the Co-operative Commonwealth Federation (CCF). This transition came about at the same time as his promotion to full professor at the University of

Toronto. Shortly after, his writings changed abruptly from the historical study
of social development in frontier Canada to a modern study of urbanization
and its consequences for urban poverty. He also became an essayist writing
on Canadian social issues and problems such as multiculturalism, social
protest and poverty.

His later analyses do not focus on the unequal development of capitalism, but tend to stress the inadequacy of hinterland values in adapting to an
industrial and urban society. He tends to dismiss Marxist ideas as "un-
Canadian" and, somewhat oddly, as American imports. He states that the best
stance for the Canadian social scientist is in the middle of the political
spectrum. He could hardly understand the student movement and denounces
it, claiming it was produced by the sons and daughters of the affluent.
According to John Conway,

> Sadly his later career came close to undoing his reputation among
> many of the present generation of sociologists. His late turn to
> American sociological methods; his continentalism and his unthink-
> ing opposition to all nationalism, even the new progressive national-
> ism which had as its aim a return to many of Clark's own original
> commitments; his fear and disdain of mass movements; his incred-
> ibly blind and hostile response to the student movements; his late
> convergence with established opinion: all served to undermine what
> could have been the greatest period in his career (1983a, 366-67).

Many members of the student movement went on to become social scientists
themselves after a spell in graduate schools and have become influential in
the Canadian sociology movement. While many are aware of the foundation
laying and cornerstone work undertaken by Clark to develop sociology in
Canada, there is often an uneasiness about Clark as an establishment figure
who produced establishment thought.

Clark's early political and social thought is radical, progressive, socialist
and collectivist and his major scholarly writings up until the late 1950s have
to be seen as reflecting the centrality of such values. There was a shift
towards a personal conservatism and scholarly accommodation of establishment sociology, but this was a development of the 1950s that did not reach
complete fruition in his published work until after 1959 (with some minor
indications first emerging in 1953). It was not until then that Clark became a
liberal individualist, and a supporter of corporate capitalism and the academic
establishment.

In the 1930s and 1940s Clark was a democratic socialist from a radical
prairie background who clearly and explicitly rejected liberal individualism
and competitive and corporate capitalism. This prairie radical socialism of

S.D. Clark has been largely hidden from critics who have come to judge him on his impact in more recent years. It can be argued that this early radical prairie socialism provided the underlying paradigmatic grounding for all his scholarly writings up to and including *Movements of Political Protest* published in 1959. It thus becomes clear that there are two Clarks: one whose sociology is infused with his early democratic socialist ideology, and a later one whose work is ideologically tinged with a conservative-Liberal outlook and an acceptance of mainstream American professionalized sociology. Since Clark's longer and pathbreaking scholarly works date from the earlier period, there is every reason for progressive Canadian sociology and the Canadian sociology movement to continue to incorporate this work into its interpretative framework.

The Young Clark in His Context

S.D. Clark was the son of a farming family living near Lloydminster, a prairie town that straddles the border of Saskatchewan and Alberta. He was born in 1910 and thus as a boy had seen the United Farmers of Alberta come to power in 1921. The farmers' revolt against the prevailing economic and political system had been going on for some time when Clark reached his twenties. Farmers formed the governments in Ontario and Manitoba, as well as in his own province, and they had become the second largest party at the federal level in 1925. (Because many of their reforms could only be effected in Ottawa, and due to their inexperience in political life, the farmers in politics were only successful to a limited degree.) The depression simply reinforced the young farm boy's conviction that the prevailing system was rigged against the real producers in society.

The beliefs of the young S.D. Clark are laid out in a series of letters to the editor of the *Lloydminster Times* in 1932 and 1933, as well as in an article in the *Canadian Forum* in 1932. He had by this time been at university for five years and had studied under such well-known academics as Hilda Neatby, A.S. Morton and R. MacGregor Dawson at the University of Saskatchewan (1927-31), and with Frank Underhill, George Brown and Chester Martin at the University of Toronto.

Clark was a wordy correspondent with the *Lloydminster Times*. He found it difficult to restrain himself as he was strongly committed to a message that he felt others needed to share. What S. Delbert Clark (as he signed himself) wrote about was a clear exposition of a socialist outlook. He did not identify himself as a Marxian communist, but did suggest that he was "a sympathizer of Communism," that "Socialism and Communism" were not "irreconcilable" (27 April 1933) and that if socialism failed, then "perhaps we shall join the ranks of Tim Buck. It won't be our fault" (14 January 1932, Tim Buck was a leader of Canadian communism). Perhaps enough has been said to point out how different S.D. Clark was at this time from the politically Liberal and less radical figure he became in the 1960s and 1970s. The system of thought that Clark espoused in the 1930s followed a coherent pattern. He suggested that the prevailing economic system only benefited "the self-interest of greedy capitalists" (18 February 1932) and the "profits of the exploiting class" (29 March 1932). In general he denounced "the inadequacy and incompetency of capitalism" (11 February 1932) and the nature of our "pernicious economic system" (18 February 1932). He pointed specifically to the predominance in modern capitalism of the financial sector. Thus he revealed how "our financial leaders . . . now enjoy despotic and regal power" (ibid.), the western countries are falling under "a financial dictatorship," and North America is falling under "the dictatorship of a financial Plutocracy" (18 August 1932). Clark believed that only by "crushing the power of finance" could "the individual assume a rightful share of the control of his destiny" (ibid.).

The political sector, for Clark, gave no relief from the dominance of economic power since, for him, the finance capitalists controlled the parliamentary and state systems. His view of the relationship between economic and political interests would be characterised today as "instrumentalist" by modern political sociologists, with the financiers directly controlling the political system. The House of Commons itself was "merely a debating forum" (28 July 1932) and the Prime Minister had "been reduced to the position of a figurehead of the financial interests" (ibid.). Clark looked back one hundred years to when there had been no such great financiers, a time when the "economic life of the country was dominated by small individualist capitalists" and the parliament was "elected by the people" (18 August 1932). In the 1930s he felt that, "Today, both functions are performed by a small group of self-appointed financiers" (ibid.). The youthful S.D. Clark vigorously denied the "pluralistic" view of political and economic life which became so influential in the political sociology of the 1950s.

Since Clark has been typified by Deborah Harrison as a liberal individualist stressing individual mobility and competition, and writing about "individuals on the make" as she puts it, it may be important to look at young Clark's comments on such matters to see whether his outlook is better described as liberal individualist or socialist collectivist. In fact, Clark denounced "economic individualism" as taught by J.S. Mill and Jeremy Bentham, claiming it had led "the world into anarchy and resulted in the chaos of an international war" (28 July 1932). He felt that social progress would be made only when "competition would be eliminated" (29 March 1932) and he denounced "the waste of competition." He felt that economic individualism and competition led to a waste of energy, such as the proverbial "four gasoline stations . . . . situated on the four corners of intersecting streets" and the "dozen commercial travellers" who competed to sell the same supplies, "the only difference in the brands being the names on the outside labels" (ibid.). He commented, "There is scarcely any end to such instances of waste in competition" (ibid.), and looked forward to the day when "private property is subordinate to the interests of the state" (ibid.). In Clark's vision, "With the realization of a Socialist Commonwealth, everyone would be producing something, not for his own pecuniary gain nor that of his nations but for the gain of civilized mankind" (11 February 1932). Such opinions fit better with the radical collectivism advocated by Harrison herself than with liberal individualism.

Clark was fearful for the future because he felt war was inevitable. He felt this not because of the actions of Germany or the threat of Nazism as such, but because the capitalists needed a war to solve the problems that were being caused by the Depression. He felt that war would help "our great industrial capitalists" (18 February 1932) in several ways. They would be able to "amass large fortunes" by producing war materials. War would also encourage a greater degree of social control as "dissatisfaction . . . will now be allayed since the malcontents and agitators will be conscripted for cannon fodder." Furthermore, "the remnants of our armies would return home disappointed, broken and lacking in spirit" no longer able to give "effective resistance to the capitalist order." Clark felt that "the financial leaders . . . realise that they must plunge the world into another great war." They had the precedent of the First World War when war "saved the situation except Russia." But Clark saw revolution was "looming in the background" since "that another war could be staged without revolution is highly unlikely"(ibid.).

Clark felt that the only solution to this grim problem was to advocate that socialism "be given another trial" as it "appears to hold out the more certain salvation for future society'"(14 January 1932). By 1933 the CCF had appeared and, according to Clark "has accepted a Socialist programme. Let us send them to Ottawa with an absolute majority" (27 April 1933).

But the success of socialism was somewhat doubtful according to Clark as "the privileged classes would wage war rather than surrender their inheritance." In addition, the popular response to a Depression was "conservative rather than radical because of the fear engendered"; fear which Clark felt was people's "most pronounced trait" (14 January 1932). Nevertheless, the effort to achieve socialism would be worthwhile since the alternative would be war and either violent revolution or continued domination of the financial plutocracy.

It must be clear from Clark's early ideology that this was no establishment figure speaking. He described himself as a firm democratic socialist and not simply a social democrat. In the context of the Canadian political culture, Clark was solidly on the left as he sympathized with the agrarian movements and was on the left wing of the CCF itself.

That the young Clark expressed such views is not so astonishing. Even before the Depression exacerbated the situation, the farmers' revolt against the established economic and political system had been going on for some decades, although it gained strength and impact after the First World War. While the social thought of S.D. Clark had been affected by his experience with urban democratic socialist and social democratic movements (for example his connection to the League for Social Reconstruction in Toronto in 1931-32), he had been imbued with the ideals and viewpoints of the farmers' revolt. The radical agrarian petite-bourgeoisie had little do with Marxist ideas directly, but many of their written documents dealing with monopoly capitalism and large scale capitalists still sound as radical as any produced by social movements in Canada[1]. As Harry Hiller has written, "Clark grew up in the midst of this agrarian political activity replete with its ideology of protest, and the leaders of the UFA [United Farmers of Alberta] such as William Wise Wood were his heroes. As a young boy, he had even kept a scrapbook about them and their ideas. Somewhat later, he also became familiar with the writings of William Irvine" (1982, 153).

William Irvine played a key if chequered role in the period of agrarian revolt which has been surveyed by Anthony Mardiros in his biography. Originally a UFA member, he came to wider notice through his book *The Farmer in Politics* published in 1920, the year before the UFA swept in to power and shut the established parties in Alberta out of power for half a century. An analysis of Irvine's thought shows how deeply the young Clark relied on this older prairie mentor.

One of Irvine's themes was the true nature of political democracy. For Irvine, "The history of Canada is the record of the rise, development, and supremacy of class rule" with the ruling class reaching a peak under the Borden government of the First World War which was "in reality nothing more than the cooperation of the plutocratic classes for the domination and exploitation of the dominion" (1920, 198). He suggested that at an earlier time some "degree of competition among the plutocratic classes" had existed, but since the emergence of the Union Government of Sir Robert Borden with its domination by "the plutocratic classes . . . every semblance of democracy vanished from Canadian life" (ibid.).

The "plutocrats" were identified as "twenty-three money kings who control the whole arterial system of Canadian commercial life." The political system, for Irvine, directly represented the wishes of the money kings. In his words, "These kings of commerce and industry are the commanders of the political parties. They dictate the policies, and they make the laws, and they do both in the sole interest of property rights and business" (1920, 202). Irvine went on to detail how much legislation was "enacted by and for our twenty-three money kings" (1920, 203) including the disposition of natural resources, and the role of the tariff (which he characterised as "of enormous benefit to manufacturers but *equally disadvantageous* to everybody else") in setting up the rights to private property above the needs for health and education of the people (1920, 204). The tariff was always of concern to farmers since it acted as an extra tax on foreign goods, thus keeping their prices artificially high. The resulting prices on foreign products helped Canadian manufacturers but hurt farmers.

For Irvine, farmers and industrial workers must organise to counter the control of parliament by "the selfishness of manufacturers" and the "plutocrats." Unless they did so, the government and its economic policy and laws would always go against the vast majority of the population who did not belong to the dominant classes. He held no modern Althusserian-Poulantzasian doctrine of the relative autonomy of the state, but instead a direct (and perhaps vulgar) instrumentalist theory of the state.

After the farmers and allied classes had taken over the government, they could set about to change the economic system, a system based on "individualism in industry" (Irvine 1920, 33), competition and profit-making. For Irvine the profit motive denied service to the community: "our competitive system is one grand race for profit-making. There are no competitors for service. Service is incidental in the industrial scheme" (1920, 29). The alternative Irvine was advocating was a system based on a radical collectivism.

As noted above, Clark felt that socialism was the only answer. Yet he feared the social contradictions of the farmers' position, especially the farmers' individualism. In words that correspond with but predated those of C.B. Macpherson in later years, he pointed out in an article that appeared in the *Canadian Forum* that it "is impossible to say whether the Western Farmers are the most radical or the most conservative people in Canada" (1932, 8). On the one hand, the farmer "remained from beginning to end an individualist— an embryo capitalist" who always sought "independence"; he or she was an entrepreneur who remained "a small capitalist in a highly capitalized world" (1932b, 7). As such, the farmer often constructed an individualist philosophy, was "almost arrogantly individualist in his outlook . . . and looked with suspicion upon cooperative effort" (1932b:7). More recently (since the traditional low-tariff Liberal Party had maintained high tariffs between 1896 and 1911), many farmers had realized that their independence "remains but a fiction" and that they were dependent on the banks, railways and farm implements companies. Because of this realization, many farmers "have now become proletarians" who have adopted a collectivist philosophy.

Clark believed that this division of opinion was unresolved, creating "a muddled and contradictory philosophy." He worried that the individualism of the majority of farmers would prevent the CCF from becoming truly socialist, pointing out that the farmers had ensured that private ownership of agricultural land would remain a CCF plank. "It is no sin for the Government to own the systems of transportation, manufacturing and banking; but the farmer must be absolute boss over his own broad fields" (Clark 1932, 8). For Clark this conservatism of farmers meant that a true socialist party could not be achieved: "In short the new Federation may be a valuable contribution to social reform; but for some time at least, it cannot be a cohesive Socialist party" (ibid.).

Clark's writings of 1932 and 1933 were essentially politically motivated. His first truly academic articles and books appeared in 1938. By this time he was a lecturer at the University of Toronto. His parents were running the family farm and would continue to do so until 1942 when his brother took over (Hiller 1982, 152). Clark retained his identification with the CCF until 1953, at which time he changed his allegiance to the Liberal Party of Canada. By 1953 he had published three of the books which contributed substantially to his reputation. The book which is arguably his best (Nock 1983, 93; Campbell 1983, 170), *Church and Sect in Canada*, was published in 1948, five years before his political break. His later book, *The Developing Canadian Community* (1963), was a collection of his more important essays, many of which had been published prior to 1953. Thus a major portion of his writing, including much of that for which he was celebrated in the world of Canadian scholarship, was published while he still considered himself to be an adherent to the democratic left. *Movements of Political Protest* appeared in 1959, but still utilized the framework he had worked out in the 1940s (although, as will be pointed out later, his shift in political stance was reflected in some subtle but important ways). It is the thesis of this chapter that the early social views of Clark, as reflected in the *Lloydminster Times,* continued to have an important influence on the subject, tone and paradigmatic approach of his more consciously academic writing until his conversion to the Liberal Party and for some time after, that is to say, until the publication of *Movements of Political Protest.*

The Young Scholar

The scholarly writings of the young Clark are academic in style and tone, and are seemingly written in the detached "neutral" voice usually adopted in academic prose. Distinctly lacking are the polemical tone and phrases that appear in his journalistic writings as a socialist advocate. Clark had learned his lessons of academic socialisation well. Yet no matter how detached the tone, the sociology of knowledge holds that a world-view and ideology stands behind all writing, including that of the social sciences (see Nock and Nelsen 1982, for a further discussion of this point). Such world-views do not (necessarily) lead a social scientist to lie or to alter facts. But he or she chooses what questions to ask, what subjects to study, and what interpretations to make of the observed facts on the basis of the world-view and ideology.

Clark's earliest publication looked into the Canadian Manufacturers Association (CMA). This interest was in evidence as early as 1933 when, following a year at the London School of Economics, he began working at the McGill Department of Sociology on his MA thesis on this subject. Harry Hiller comments, "The selection of this topic for the focus of his M.A. research in sociology was also consonant with his historical and economic interests even if it was not very sociological in the Chicago tradition. In spite of his exposure to Dawsonian sociology (McGill's senior sociology professor), the thesis turned out to be very unecological and was clearly an exception to the emphasis in McGill's program" (1982, 46). He continued to work on the CMA for his PhD dissertation in the Department of Political Economy at Toronto from 1935 to 1938.

Given his radical agrarian and democratic socialist background, this was a logical and perhaps even an inspired choice. It was the tariff issue more than any other single issue which had consistently annoyed farmers. They were convinced that a high protection tariff kept them in poverty, resulted in ruinously high prices, caused rapid depopulation of rural areas because of the ruin of farmers unable to pay artificially high prices, produced social problems in the city because of the swelling of the urban population, and resulted in the emergence of an employee society, sometimes referred to by the farmers as the "new feudalism." To the modern reader, the tariff might seem an important but dry and technical issue. However, it was an issue that rallied most farmers to a common cause, from moderate farm leaders such as T.C. Crerar and E.C. Drury to more radical leaders such as William Irvine.

The issue led many farmers to the conclusion that both old-line parties were unresponsive to the popular demands placed upon them and that the older parties had "sold out" to the plutocratic classes (although the more moderate leaders always seemed to hold out the hope that the Liberal Party, which had started life at least in part as a farmer-supported low tariff party, might return to the fold and see the light). In turn, this led to the demand for group representation by which farmers and workers would represent their own interests directly instead of being minor players in parties which were dominated by the money kings or even by liberal professionals. Thus, combined with his agrarian background, a study of the CMA would tell Clark much about how and why farmers had been excluded from influence in the political system. Obviously such a topic would also appeal to an urban socialist as the manufacturers were seen by the socialist movement as of central importance in modern capitalism—with such exemplars as the Fords. Clark's chosen topic allowed him to observe just how much influence manufacturing capitalists had in the political system.

Clark was very interested in the issues surrounding the tariff, the lobbying of the CMA, and the resulting union of purpose between the government and manufacturers. As Clark suggests "Dependence tended to be placed upon the lobbyist rather than upon the industrial engineer or sales promoter; the struggle for higher tariffs or bounties provided a rallying point which brought manufacturers together. These privileges established the close connection of the manufacturing industries with the government" (1938, 506).

Clark analysed the ideology behind the CMA and its tactics. It practiced neutrality and nonpartisanship in relations with the two old parties but actively favoured parties supporting a high tariff. The Association tended to identify its own need for a high tariff with the national interest, while denouncing farmer-labour movements. For example, a president of the CMA said, "We do not want warring groups in Canada but rather a union of all groups to advance the interests of our common country" (Clark 1938, 514).

A second article by Clark looks directly at "the CMA and the tariff" and states bluntly, "Protection as an economic creed has been largely an expression of industrial capitalism in Canada" (1939, 19). "The tariff systems developed with the growth of [the] manufacturing industry and it was pressed upon the Government as a necessary policy by organizations formed to advance the interests of manufacturers" (ibid., 19). Clark went on to defend this thesis with a myriad of details. Such an argument obviously was in harmony with Clark's radical agrarian background.

In *The Social Development of Canada* (1942) Clark presented an analysis which he was later to elaborate more fully in religious and political contexts. What had to be explained, as Clark saw it, was the tendency for frontier populations to reject traditional institutions and methods of social organization. Frontier populations tended to see monopolistic institutions supported by the state as "coercive controls" and as "privileged" (Clark 1942, 5). Whether the subject at hand was an established church, trading companies granted royal charters, or the leadership of "family compacts" of politically connected and nepotistic kin, the frontier settlers saw such developments as encroachments on their own liberty. Social innovation was natural on the frontier as these populations were "less dependent upon traditional institutions even after they were established" (1942, 6). Farmers who supported and recruited circuit-riding preachers, for example, might be less than enthusiastic to see one-seventh of all land given over to the Church of England for its maintenance. Small French-Canadian fur traders resented the monopoly given to royal-chartered companies and resisted what they saw as an unjust imposition from a state which seemed alien to their interests. Thus on the frontier, "nonconformist attitudes," "habits of independence" and "new patterns of behaviour" emerged which combated "traditional systems of institutional control" (ibid.). Such forces on the frontier produced "the weaknesses of economic monopolies, colonial class systems, established churches, or authoritarian systems of government" (1942, 7). All such traditional institutions were introduced but were resisted by frontier residents. Clark concludes, "the newly developing Canadian communities . . . were outcasts of some sort from older societies" (ibid.).

Given the resentment felt by the frontier population regarding the alien state, it was natural that reformers and even "social revolutionists" emerged on the frontier to challenge what Clark called the "vested interests." While Clark realized that a variety of factors, from the "boredom of routine tasks" to the "love of power," might influence such leaders, he emphasized that they could only succeed with community support. Clark stressed that "the reformer differed from the 'crank' in that he gave expression to genuine and persistent social needs and dissatisfactions" and that it was "this need for social expression" experienced by the community "rather than the character or motives of reformers which gave rise to reform movements" (1942, 15). By 1954, Clark much more readily viewed such frontier leaders as lacking in "political intelligence" (1962, 218) and as representing "not a rich and progressive but a poor and retarded society" (ibid.). In this earlier work, however, the frontier reformers and radicals are presented as logical responses to the more or less just objections of frontier populations to alien bureaucratic and monopolistic states which burdened rather than aided the frontier population.

The appeal of such an analysis to the young Clark should be clear. He had grown up in a period of constant agrarian and frontier unrest. It must have seemed almost natural for such a population to be at odds with conventional society. As a boy and young man, for example, he had seen the UFA and Social Credit supplant the Liberal and Conservative parties. His student, W.E. Mann, later wrote a book outlining the strengths of sects in Alberta as opposed to the relative weakness of more conventional denominations and churches (1955). In exploring the frontier protest against the monopolistic state and traditionalistic institutions from the time of the French regime to the settlement of the prairies at the turn of the century, Clark was also studying the nature of the social forces which had led to the ubiquitousness of reformist and revolutionary movements on all of the Canadian frontiers, right down to his own Alberta.

In his early writings Clark denounces the plutocratic classes. He comes back to this theme rather pointedly in his major work *Church and Sect in Canada (1948)*. This is a study which ranges in time from 1760 almost to his own day, and from Nova Scotia westward to William Aberhart's Alberta. Each chapter centres on the social significance of religious affiliation in hinterland areas. In each new area of settlement on the frontier, there was an effort in Canada by the dominant classes emanating from Britain to support religious bodies which reflect their own establishment views. Such a religion as espoused by the dominant classes was relatively unemotional, hierarchical and patriarchal in its organization, and laid considerable stress on the expertise and education expected of men of God. In provinces such as Ontario and Nova Scotia, there was also a direct process of affiliating the church and state as had been the case in Britain itself.

Most settlement frontiers were inhabited by uneducated men and women who not infrequently had left (even fled) the older settled areas of Europe and the Americas for a more democratic milieu where people could expect to own land individually rather than be tenants or worse for aristocratic landowners; thus, it was not surprising that church-forms of religion seemed culturally inappropriate, and politically and socially symbolic of the dominant classes trying to spread their control. The sects, with their greater emotional appeal, with their emphasis on a personal call from God that could override formal training and studies and the costs of advanced education, with their democratic rather than hierarchical and episcopal organization, naturally had greater appeal. As Michael S. Cross puts it:

> S.D. Clark . . . gives a broad spectrum approach, relating the conflict of the established churches and the evangelical sects to the nature of the frontier society, and linking it to other challenges to traditional institutions—particularly the rejection of the British class system and the frontier reaction against undemocratic forms of government. In discussing what he considers the failure of the traditional churches to provide the social leadership needed by a frontier society, to develop 'a more inclusive philosophy,' Clark seems to come down squarely as a supporter of the evangelicals and their democratic approaches. As with the orthodox frontierists, then, there is a strong moral content to his history (1970, 80-81).

In his introduction to *Church and Sect in Canada*, Clark points out that some large religious denominations,

> have struggled to secure a dominant position. Some of them have enjoyed the protection and assistance of the state. All of them have had the support of powerful economic and social interests . . . . Throughout the development of Canada, from the early settlement of New France to the present day, undercurrents of unrest in religious organisations have found expression in the break from established religious authority and in the emergence of new religious forms.

A good example of this process was the fuss caused by the ministry of Henry Alline, the son of a New England farmer who had settled in Nova Scotia in the 1770s. As an uneducated frontier farmer, Alline would not have been of good enough background to obtain the education needed for ordination from the established churches, but his direct call from God meant he could bypass the worldly and ecclesiastical authorities. According to Alline, "Although many (to support the ministry of Antichrist) will pretend there is no such thing as a man's knowing in these days he is called to preach any other way than by his going to the seats of learning to be prepared for the ministry, and then authorized by men: yet blessed by God, there is a knowledge of these things, which an educated man knows nothing of" (Clark 1948, 21). As Clark comments, "In responding to this call, he challenged the prerogative of the Church to perform ordination." Alline's perspective is clear, "I saw I needed nothing to qualify me but Christ" (Clark 1948, 21).

As a settlement matured, as the outside metropolis asserted its control, as a greater degree of socioeconomic differentiation created greater degrees of wealth and poverty, the population was more likely to be incorporated into the wider system of authority. The frontier moved west (or, at least, away in a different direction) and the same process began anew.

The subject matter of *Church and Sect in Canada* surely appealed to the agrarian radical that Clark had been and still was. In such works he explored the radical and deviant roots of agrarian and frontier communities from the past and sought to grapple with why such periods of unrest always seemed to pass on and why former areas of unrest, such as the Maritime Provinces, were relatively quiescent by his own time. *Church and Sect in Canada* could be seen as the logical outcome of the combining of Clark's early political and social views and his academic influences. As an academic personally interested in movements which question the status quo, it is not surprising that he should study other times and places which have undergone similar struggles or movements.

The Epistemological Break in S.D. Clark
It may be of interest to take a close look at a paper Clark presented to the annual meeting of the Royal Society of Canada in 1954, a year after he decided to support the Liberal Party of Canada. It cannot be accidental that, for the first time in Clark's published work, there is a note of doubt and even of condemnation of the radical agrarian movements. In talking about his home province of Alberta, where twenty-two years earlier he had been fanning the flames of protest in a rather supportive milieu, he now committed to print before his intellectual peers this judgement:

We have been too much inclined perhaps to exaggerate the political intelligence of frontier populations. It comes hard to one brought up in Alberta to suggest that the people of that province who thought of themselves as in the vanguard of reform actually had only a limited appreciation of the complexities of modern government and no great understanding of the conditions necessary for the preservation of individual rights and a sense of community responsibility. In a cultural sense, the frontier was not a rich and progressive but a poor and retarded society' (Clark 1962, 219).

Clark points out that political reform was "only one of many forms of frontier protest which also included medical quackery, vigilantism, mob rioting." He goes on to suggest that what characterised the UFA was "an underlying attitude of irresponsibility with respect to the larger affairs of the community," and even indicates that the UFA sought to make the individual "in a sense a poor citizen" and that "poor citizenship" became with the Social Credit "almost a condition of membership of the party" (ibid.).

Later in this essay, Clark portrays McCarthyism in the USA as a logical outcome of American radical agrarian radicalism. Thus he writes, "The attack of Joseph McCarthy upon communist influences in the government of the United States was a clear and genuine expression of the American frontier, isolationist spirit. It was no accident that McCarthy came from the Middle West and represented an ethnic-religious minority population in the United States" (1962, 216). These words, delivered in 1954, surely tell us more about the mind of S.D. Clark than about the McCarthy phenomenon. After all, Wisconsin in the 1950s was hardly on the edge of any frontier, and McCarthy, a Roman Catholic, did not come from the hard sectarian Protestantism that Clark himself had characterised as a natural development of the frontier.

This new rejection of a more radical or socialist viewpoint is also in evidence in Clark's foreword in C.B. Macpherson's *Democracy in Alberta: Social Credit and the Party System* (1953). In his 1932 *Canadian Forum* article, Clark voices a number of ideas which were similar to those of Macpherson. Macpherson and Clark were colleagues in the Department of Political Economy at the University of Toronto. Macpherson, while strictly academic in his writings, has usually been connected with the left, even the Marxist viewpoint and as such provides a class-based and materialistic explanation of the appeal of the Social Credit to a party of farmers who retained land ownership and a sense of entrepreneurship in their ideology. The older Clark reveals his doubts regarding Macpherson's perspective. He suggests contentiously that, "Not all Professor Macpherson's readers will accept his conclusions, but this is not the place to question the arguments put forward" (1953, vii). Earlier he also casts doubt by stating, "However far one may be prepared to go in accepting Professor Macpherson's explanations . . . ."

Evidently Clark is no longer prepared to go the whole distance with Macpherson's class-based analysis.

Although the general Clarkian framework remains in his last major work which owes something to his own agrarian origin *(Movements of Political Protest in Canada, 1640-1840)*, the shift in orientation is also clear in this text when Clark suggests that the frontier encouraged "a system of political irresponsibility" (1959, 8). In discussing frontier insurgents such as Papineau, Mackenzie and Aberhart, Clark describes them as "irresponsible" (1959, 505) although he does acknowledge that such leaders might "be seeking a better world to live in" (1959, 505).

Despite the major shift in Clark's views towards a questioning of frontier radicalism, his own interpretation remains largely that which he had constructed earlier. In *Movements of Political Protest in Canada, 1640-1840*, the emphasis is on looking at the "revolutionary forces" that had affected Canadian political development. According to Clark, "On the North American continent political authority was established only in face of almost continuous resistance on the part of the population in outlying areas'"(1959, 4). New areas of settlement "organized their own systems of control, and when central authority sought to establish itself, movements of revolt quickly developed" (ibid.) Against the state, dominated by the longer settled areas usually back east, the frontier exhibited an "intense localism" of almost "sectarian exclusiveness" (1959, 5). The state was costly to pioneers who could largely do without it, with their dependence either on local individualism or community co-operation. Like the state church, the state itself was seen as a costly and alien intrusion. Thus Clark states, "Reform on the frontier was directed against such social evils of the outside world as political patronage, the payment of excessive salaries to government officials, economic monopoly, a stringent money supply, exorbitant interest charges, and burdensome taxation" (ibid.).

In the context of Canada, such frontier revolts against the state involved disloyalty to European powers which, up until 1840, still attempted to control the new areas of frontier development with forms of social organisation imported from a more rigidified class and state system. Clark's analysis of the rebellions of 1837-1838 in Lower and Upper Canada takes up about half the book. Other authors have described these rebellions as contests for responsible government, but Clark sees them as having, "the object of liberating the Canadian population from British rule . . . of freeing the population of British North America from the rule of an overseas power" (1959, 255). For Clark, these movements were by no means ones supported for individual gain, but "were very real and genuinely appealing" to frontier settlers "who, suspicious of the Federal power in the United States, were even more suspicious of the powers of an overseas empire" (1959, 256).

An interesting example of Clark's analysis is that of the Patriote rebellion in Lower Canada. Some authorities hold that this was interpreted as a war between the ethnic groups or "races" (as the older usage had it). More recently Fernand Ouellet has suggested it was due to the narrow socioeconomic self-interest of a liberal professional class whose mobility was blocked and who used a nationalistic appeal to further their own narrow views. Donald Creighton, another prominent authority on this subject, suggests the liberal professionals stood in the way of the progressive business community in Montreal because their aims were threatened by this business class. Both authors tend to deny the truly popular nature and significance of the rebellions in their focus on a small elite's class self-interest.

Clark's analysis remains based on the notion that frontier populations were struggling to overcome the coercive power of an oppressive state system that owed its existence to a foreign European imperialism. For Clark, then, the Patriote movement was a genuine response by the rural population, and not simply the elite's manipulation by French Canadian liberal professionals.

By the mid to late 1950s Clark had moved a long way from his origins. He lived in Central Canada and taught at the University of Toronto. He joined a party that has always chosen its leaders from Québec and Ontario, the Liberal Party of Canada. He was a member of the Royal Society of Canada, which had been founded by a Governor General of Canada who had been a member of the British aristocracy (ironically just the sort of authority Clark critiques in his academic writings on resistance to the British class system). Of course, the times were so much better and the state had, with the Keynesian revolution, become an active state with many social benefit programs. As Hiller puts it, "The optimism that was part of the post-war era was particularly maintained by persons like Clark who had experienced the hardships of the depression years" (Hiller 1982, 156). The fortunes of Canada's protest parties suffered. In some cases, as with the Social Credit, the movement ceased to be a movement of protest at all, and simply became another big business party.

Clark's early socialist radicalism had been predicated on the view that capitalism could not recover and that a war would produce a revolution or a situation worse than the 1930s. Neither of these things had happened and prosperity was general, unemployment low. In addition, Clark was far from Alberta and by now was a long-time resident of Toronto. As Hiller says, "It is important to note that his commitment to socialism was born in agrarian populism rather than industrial radicalism, and . . . the more Clark became removed from that agrarian environment in time and space, the more his enthusiastic zeal for it waned" (1982, 155). It is likely that Clark's turning away from topics which had been of such burning interest to a prairie radical also occurred because of his altered political, social and physical environment.

Throughout the 1960s and 1970s (and starting in the 1950s with his shift to the Liberal Party), Clark's social outlook increasingly supported the authority structures of his society. It was at this time that large numbers of activists from the Canadian sociology movement entered sociology departments as doctoral students and professors. These students were confused about the nature of Clark's heritage. The conservatism of his present outlook (and his Liberalism in politics), the general difficulty for sociology readers of his main works, and some of his actions during the fiercer days of the late 1960s and early 1970s, tended to produce doubt about whether Clark's writings could or should be incorporated as part of a progressive Canadian sociology, and whether they were compatible or hostile to a materialistic and neo-Marxist outlook. The subject matter of the new Marxist sociology often also tended to be different from Clark's concerns. Much of the new Marxist sociology was directed to understanding Canada's place and fate *vis-a-vis* the juggernaut of American imperialist capitalism. In this view, the Canadian state was accepted as a given, and movements which might threaten the Canadian state and which thereby might weaken resistance to the American threat could be interpreted in a hostile light. Thus it is evident that S.D. Clark's early writing up to 1959 (with exceptions as noted after 1953) needs to be prefaced with a proper understanding of his own agrarian radicalism and socialism to be understood.

It is my argument that Clark's early work must be incorporated into the new Canadian progressive sociology and social science. Clark's subject matter remains of importance to a progressive Canadian sociology— the rejection of the British and French class system and system of authority and social control (such as the established church, aristocratic landowners), the vitality of movements of political and social protest on the frontier, the importance of the farmer's movement, and the nature and functioning of Canadian manufacturers and capitalists are highly significant aspects of our history. The fact that Clark became socially more conservative and politically more Liberal in his outlook from 1953 onward should not be allowed to obscure the importance of the writings of the early Clark witten from the paradigmatic outlook and ideology of an agrarian radical democratic socialist.

Note
[1] David Laycock has provided the best overall analysis of radical prairie movements in his Populism and Democratic Thought in the Canadian Prairies, 1910 to 1945. He identifies "crypto-Liberalism," Radical Democratic, Social Democratic and Social Credit forms of populism and points out that despite differences in the points of view of these traditions "each variant cohere(d) around principles concerning redistribution of power among social classes and groups" (Laycock 1990, 4).

Chapter Three

S.D. Clark and the Rebellions of 1837-38

The Rebellions of 1837-38 have become an important component of the collective memory which Canadians have of themselves, an essential element of "the sacred history" of the nation as Mircea Eliade (1963, 5) would call it. Perhaps it is quintessentially Canadian that there exist very polarized views on the significance of the Rebellions and their leaders for future developments in Canadian society. These polarized views run the gamut from Charles Lindsey's favourable 1862 two-volume biography of William Lyon Mackenzie to Colin Read's impressive conservative reinterpretation of the Duncombe Revolt in western Ontario. That these diverse interpretations have survived the transition from amateur and even filiopietistic to modern "scientific" academic historical research, and even to quantitative methods such as espoused by Fernand Ouellet and Colin Read, suggests that what are at issue are paradigmatic interpretations of the past which are relatively resistant to empirical disconfirmation (Kuhn 1962). E.H. Carr reminds us that the study of history is not simply an exercise dealing with an external reality, but one in which the interaction between the external world of reality and the internal world of the historian is primary. He writes,

> The historian starts with a provisional selection of facts, and a provisional interpretation in the light of which that selection has been made—by others as well as by himself. As he works, both the interpretation and the selection of facts undergo subtle and perhaps partly unconscious changes, through the reciprocal action of one or the other. And this reciprocal action also involves reciprocity between present and past, since the historian is part of the present and the facts belong to the past . . . . My first answer therefore to the question "What is history?" is that it is a continuous process of interaction between the historian and his [or her] facts, an unending dialogue between the present and the past (Carr 1961, 30).

Carl Berger, in writing about the progressive historians of the United States points out their "view of historical knowledge as relative to time and circumstance" and that "the ideal of objective history was impatiently dismissed as an impossible anachronism" (1976, 62). Frank Underhill, a close friend and mentor of S.D. Clark, wrote in 1932, "The historian must ever endeavour to be conscious and critical of his own system of values, but he cannot escape from it or from the dominant ideas of his own age. The patterns which he finds in the events of the past are the image of the patterns which are already in his own mind" (ibid.).

The concern of this chapter is the interpretation of S.D. Clark's ideas on the 1837 Rebellions and their 1838 aftermath as expressed in his major work *Movements of Political Protest in Canada, 1640-1840* (1959). This is the final volume in the pathbreaking Social Credit in Alberta series funded by the Rockefeller Foundation with Clark himself as general editor. It is also the last substantial and sustained use by Clark of his qualitative historical sociology approach, and of his marriage of the frontier thesis and the Chicago School's theory of social disorganization and reorganization. *Movements of Political Protest* is an imposing work which, as its title suggests, goes far beyond the Rebellions of 1837 in scope. Nevertheless, about half of the book is taken up with discussing the Rebellions; clearly Clark felt they were of major significance to the nature of Canadian social development.

As a preface to examining Clark's interpretation of the Rebellions it is useful to consider the tools we are about to use. Within sociology itself, the sociology of knowledge has emerged as a field explicitly concerned with exploring the connections between the production of knowledge and its social genesis. The sociology of knowledge contains "the recognition that knowledge in the *broadest sense* is context dependent and somehow con-strained by social factors" (Stehr and Meja 1984, 1). As "a recognized *speciality,*" the sociology of knowledge has flourished since the late 1920s, although as Nico Stehr and Volker Meja point out, "its subject matter has always been a major part of the intellectual domain of sociology itself" (1984, 1). Regarding one of the most central questions, that of the problem of relativism, one of the most influential replies has been to assert that there is no final basis for certainty which can obviate the influences of the social milieu. In referring to a number of their contributors, Stehr and Meja point to "the central tenet of the sociology of knowledge, to wit: that there is no privileged site of speech but instead a field of perpetual conflict between partial perspectives wherein consciousness is socially rooted . . ." (1984, 21). My goal is not to disprove or prove in any positivistic sense, what S.D. Clark has written on the Rebellions of 1837, nor do I think that this is possible.

The Rebellions of 1837-38 and their Interpretation

Rather my first aim is to demonstrate that (a) as far as explanations of the Rebellions are concerned, it would have been just as logical, on the basis of the evidence, for Clark to have opposed as to have supported the significance of the Rebellions for Canadian social development; and (b) Clark's positive evaluations of the significance of the Rebellions were bound up with his academic affiliations and with his radical agrarian formation as a young rural populist and socialist.

Clark starts off by discussing the contention that Canada "in contrast with the United States, has no revolutionary tradition" (1959, 3). This he claims is untrue: Canada has indeed had revolutions but "they have been largely unsuccessful." Because of their ill success, Canadians tend to forget their revolutions, to condemn the leaders of such enterprises as "misguided individuals out of accord with their fellow Canadian" and to designate these revolutions as second-rate affairs led by comic opera heroes. The tendency has been to explain Canadian development in light of theories which stress the importance of the country's continued ties with Europe, rather than with the environmental and social influences of the North American setting. Clark rejects the view that "Canada . . . grew out of the political experience of nineteenth-century Europe" (1959, 4) and adopts instead the frontier perspective. He writes that the view that Canadian development is attributable to Europe "overlooks as Turner emphasized a half-century ago the way in which the principles of American government reflect the political experience of American frontier people." What Clark seeks to assert is that "Canada shared in this frontier experience" and that "any explanation of Canadian political development must take this fact into account" (ibid.).

As discussed in Chapter Two, Clark claims that frontier areas of settlement tend to produce a state of social disorganization in which the normal mechanisms of social control are absent or present only in a weakened fashion. The frontier bred a sense of resentment against the external metropolis and dominant classes as, in the eyes of frontier settlers, the state was in the control of the metropolis and tended to be costly and oppressive without providing any needed service. According to Clark, "The dominant urge of frontier populations was to be left alone, to escape the exactions and restrictions of outside political authority" (1959, 5). State and society, instead of being complementary, were antagonistic because the state represented one civilization (hierarchical British) while the society (minus the dominant classes) represented the more egalitarian American ethos promoted by the frontier. For Clark, the tragedy—which arrested the potential vigour of Canadian social development was that the social forces represented by the state kept in check and impeded the progressive social forces behind the wider society.

In addition to these assumptions, Clark holds a number of operating principles in his analysis of the Rebellions of 1837. The first is that the Rebellions truly represented the wishes of the great majority of people, shaped as they were by the common influence of the frontier; the second is that the leaders of the Rebellions were representative leaders cast up by the wider social movement rather than idiosyncratic individualists acting on their own. Regarding the first operating principle, it is by no means a foregone conclusion that the reformers always represented the majority of the population as the Clark thesis maintains.

A recent historian, Colin Read, has opined:

> To argue that many Upper Canadians harboured this or that griev-ance is not to suggest that all the aggrieved were dissatisfied with the general situation and in the camp of the reformers. It is reveal-ing to look at the four elections to the assembly in the period from 1828-1836. . . . They were far from uniformly successful, winning the contests of 1828 and 1834, but losing those of 1830 and 1836 to the Tories. Rather than proving that in the years leading up to the rebellions the reformers grew from strength to strength until they had the mass of the electorate behind them, these results show that the electorate wavered in its support of the Reformers and Tories, favouring first one, then the other (Read 1982, 7).

Read's observations do not "disprove" Clark's assumption, but illustrate that to maintain that the frontier was as important a factor as Clark be-lieved it to have been, it is necessary to argue that the frontier shaped most settlers in the Canadas in such a way as to be supportive of the Reformers. Clark does this when he suggests "the political development of the two countries [Canada and the United States] has been shaped by very similar forces" (Clark 1959, 4) and "conditions in Canada [on the frontier] com-pelled a way of life and bred a way of thinking in many respects similar to the way of life and thinking across the border" (1959, 258). He asserts that the "general support of the movement clearly developed out of sentiments and feelings deeply imbedded in the thinking of the population" (1959, 257), that the developments of 1838 showed the Rebellions were, in fact, in accord with "the real sentiments of the population" (ibid.) and that there was "strong support of the patriot cause" (1959, 258). Other historians, sociologists and critics have evaluated the same events quite differently.

As W.L. Morton suggests, Clark's "thesis tends to emphasize environ-ment rather than institutions, and to be deterministic rather than contingent. . . . In the opinion of this reviewer, the frontier in the American sense was not typical but atypical of Canadian development, and to use the thesis as an American might do is impossible for a Canadian" (1960, 243). For Morton, the Rebellions "were as much British or Irish as American, and perhaps as much urban as agrarian . . . there was really nothing in Upper Canada in 1837 that the Chartists were not to attempt in Great Britain two years later. Indeed, the whole British background of institutions and radical movements is at least as persistent as the American example in the agitation from 1827 to 1837" (1960, 244).

The Chartists were radical urban members of the British working class who demanded extension of the franchise and other improvements at a time when the industrial working class in Britain still suffered from long hours of work (ten or twelve hours a day, six days a week), low wages and denial of civil rights and benefits. By suggesting that the Chartist spirit underlay Canadian developments, W.L. Morton attacked both Clark's emphasis on their rural frontier origins and their North American locus, and indicated that the Canadian revolutionaries were just as affected by the ideals of the British urban proletariat.

Clark's paradigmatic focus also necessitated that he highlight the representativeness of the Rebellion leaders rather than view them as opportunistic or idiosyncratic and self-serving. If Upper Canada "was still very much a frontier community and it was the demands of a frontier population which found expression in the movements leading to rebellion" (Clark 1959, 331), then the movement leaders were created by the frontier setting rather than by shaping the movement themselves.

This view is evident in Clark's earlier work, *The Social Development of Canada*, but began to change during the 1950s, the decade which saw him drop his more radical commitments. However, because his more recent critical attitude was at odds with the paradigmatic needs of his argument, it was played down in *Movements of Political Protest*. His more critical and conservative attitude to the reform leadership come out more clearly in his 1954 article, "The Frontier in the Development of the Canadian Political Community," which was reprinted in *The Developing Canadian Community*, 1962.

W.G. Ormsby commented in a review, "The point that we have tended to dismiss our rebels too lightly is well taken, but William Lyon Mackenzie cannot be transformed into the typical Upper Canadian" (1960, 130). The thrust of Clark's argument was the inevitable nature of the conflict, seen as a result of the ecology and its interaction with social forces. In such a view, the leadership would tend to be interpreted as being cast up by the reform movement itself, rather than being responsible for creating, to some degree, the desire for reform. It is this point which is emphasized by Ormsby.

He goes on to suggested that Clark's argument depends upon the view that a majority of the population wanted reform, a view he holds to be unproven (1960, 130).

Up until the 1920s, a rather positive view of the Rebellions and of their leaders was commonly held in Canadian intellectual life. This positive evaluation was based upon the celebration of the achievement of "responsible government" in 1849, and the assumption that the Rebellions and their leaders were key agents in forcing the matter onto the British political agenda. No Rebellion, no responsible government, went the theme. A.B. McKillop writes that the winning of political freedom had "been construed largely as a Liberal achievement" and that "this conclusion, understandably, increased with each successive electoral triumph of the Liberal party" (1979, xiii). By 1902, Charles G.D. Roberts was even willing to conclude that the beginnings of a literary spirit in Canada also dated back to the triumph of responsible government. He wrote, "That struggle had broadened men's minds and taught them to think for themselves" (McKillop 1979, xiii).

In the 1920s this near-consensus was breached by a number of historians. They included Aileen Dunham and Chester Martin. Aileen Dunham received her BA from the University of Alberta in 1920, and her MA in 1921 from the University of Toronto. She went to the University of London for her doctoral studies which she completed in 1924. Her research for that degree was published as *Political Unrest in Upper Canada 1815-1836* in the Imperial Studies series, sponsored by the Royal Empire Society (1927). Dr Dunham taught at the College of Wooster in Ohio for many years and eventually received a named Chair—the Michael O. Fisher Professorship.

Dr Dunham noted that the years following 1837 were "fertile years" in political development (1963, 18), but the period she studied was "barren of achievement in the field of political reform." As for the Rebellions themselves, Dr Dunham was entirely dismissive, seeing them as "not a climax, but rather an anti-climax, accidental rather than inevitable and out of harmony with the *real* sentiments of Upper Canadians" (1963, 18). She felt the radical leaders of the Rebellions were "the most unbalanced element among the reformers" (ibid.). Thus Dr Dunham concluded her account with the dismissal of Sir Francis Bond Head's first parliament in the summer of 1836 because the heroes, in her eyes, were the moderate reformers prior to 1837 and the liberal British reformers such as Durham and others after 1838. She felt Canadian political development was not at all enhanced by "the extreme radicals" and she stated her "deliberate purpose" was to avoid giving leaders of the Rebellions a prominence which she felt they did not deserve.

Perhaps it was important that Chester Martin followed up Aileen Dunham's paradigmatic interpretation with his own volume, *Empire and Commonwealth: Studies in Governance and Self-Government in Canada* (1929), given that Dr Dunham was a female scholar at a small American college and thus likely in such a day and age to be overlooked and ignored. Martin was born in 1882, attended the University of New Brunswick and won the first Rhodes Scholarship given in North America (Berger 1976, 34). He studied at Balliol College, Oxford, and worked for two years at the Public Archives in Ottawa. He taught at the University of Manitoba from 1909 to 1929 and then went to Toronto where he spent the rest of his career until his retirement in 1952 as Head of the Department of History.

Martin continued Aileen Dunham's dismissal of the rebellions and its leaders by his worship of the moderate reformers such as Howe, Baldwin, Lafontaine, and Lord Elgin. Writing from the perspective of the mid 1970s, Carl Berger writes:

> The most remarkable aspect of Martin's analysis of the background to the winning of responsible government was his complete neglect of the rebellion in Upper and Lower Canada and of such radical figures as Mackenzie and Papineau. The rebellions appeared to him as unfortunate aberrations in an otherwise steady evolutionary pattern . . . Responsible government was won by . . . men of moderation who worked for short-range goals (1976, 36).

When S.D. Clark came to the University of Toronto in 1931-32 for doctoral study he took some of his courses from Chester Martin (Hiller 1982, 44). Already influenced by "his interests in the agrarian protest movements, particularly the United Farmers of Alberta," Harry Hiller notes that Clark "began to rebel against the constitutional history that Martin was emphasizing, feeling that economic history was more basic" (1982, 44-45). Douglas F. Campbell adds that Clark described 1931-32 as "his wild year, during which he read Marx, Engels, and North American left-wing writers such as Beard and Myers" (1983, 141). Campbell also points out that this was the year of his "disillusionment with the constitutional-political brand of history so popular up to that time, and of which Chester Martin was a leading exponent" (ibid.). When Clark suggested he wanted to do a thesis on the Western farmer's movement, he was told "that that topic was not history" (ibid.).

Clark was never very thorough by modern sociological standards in explaining which authors his analyses sustained or criticized. However, a close reading of *Movements of Political Protest*, reveals that Clark quotes from Aileen Dunham's conclusion that the Rebellion "was not a climax, but rather an anti-climax . . . and out of harmony with the real sentiments of Upper Canadians" (1963, 5). Such a conclusion strikes directly at Clark's own frontier analysis. He counters it by shifting the spotlight back to 1838. He writes:

> If the action at Montgomery's tavern only is considered, there might appear some reason for considering the Upper Canadian rebellion an anti-climax to the political developments of the preceding twenty-one years, and, though the fighting at St. Denis, St. Charles, and St. Eustache was of a more determined character than that which took place on the northern outskirts of Toronto, the rebellion in Lower Canada as well in terms simply of the engagements might be thought of as anti-climactical; indeed, it may be questioned whether what happened in 1837 was a rebellion at all in view of the fact that the action of the population was confined to resisting the arrest of its leaders and that the offensive was taken by the forces of the government. The developments during the year 1838 make clear, however, that in neither Upper nor Lower Canada were the occurrences in the late autumn of 1837 in any true sense anti-climactical, accidental, or out of harmony with the real sentiments of the population. The anti-climax came not in 1837 but ten years later with the attainment of responsible government (Clark 1959, 257).

Clark turns Dunham's argument about the unpopularity of the Rebellions upside down and argues that "the general support of the movement clearly developed out of sentiments and feelings deeply imbedded in the thinking of the population" (ibid.).

This is the only explicit acknowledgement of the views of either Dunham or Martin. Clark's own predisposition may be recognized by his reliance on Charles Lindsey's biography of William Lyon Mackenzie (1862). Lindsay was a son-in-law of Mackenzie and his works have a filiopietistic tone. Dunham has observed that the work was written "by a sympathetic kinsmen" and that "The work errs in interpretation rather than presentation of the facts; its sins are of omission rather than of distortion." Dunham refers to Lindsey's later book on Mackenzie (1909)—which so shockingly replaced that of Le Sueur (McKillop 1979) in the Makers of Canada series—as "An idealized character sketch" (1963, 204). Le Sueur's initial volume on Mackenzie was dropped because of pressure exerted by relatives, including Mackenzie King.

Despite Lindsey's known commitment, Clark cites his work frequently. It seems remarkable that Clark did not cite or quote Chester Martin directly, although a number of his paradigmatic comments may refer to Martin in a veiled fashion. Clark's statement, "Responsible government developed in reaction rather than in response to the true democratic spirit of the Canadian people" (1959, 4) rejects Chester Martin's assertion, "The political traditions culminating in Canadian nationhood are now the oldest in the American hemisphere—the only political traditions unbroken by a revolution or civil war" (Martin 1929).

Thus, as of the 1920s two distinct interpretations of the impact of the Rebellions of 1837 existed in Canadian historiography. One held that they acted as the impetus in achieving responsible government, while the other saw them as an unnecessary deviation from the path of moderation and state building. Although specific points may be verified by empirical evidence, in a general sense these theoretical paradigmatic interpretations are not easily falsifiable. One may adopt either perspective without fear of it being easily disproven. At the bottom of all these ways of looking at the Rebellion of 1837 are, as Underhill tells us, "the patterns which are already in [the scholars] own mind" (Berger 1976, 23).

The Social Context of Clark's Interpretation
What then explains S.D. Clark's interpretation of the Rebellions if it is not simply a clear-cut use of the evidence? It would seem logical to expect that Clark's exposure to Chester Martin in 1931-32 would have led him to adopt Martin's own position in favour of moderation over any violent attempts at social change. Since Martin was Head of the Department of History and remained an important university figure at Toronto even after Clark's conversion to political economy and sociology, it might have been prudent and advantageous to adopt such views. Yet Clark did not do so.

Perhaps Clark's interpretation of the Rebellions of 1837, as a scholar, must be explained not in terms of the weight of "factual objective" evidence, although that always plays a role, but in terms of his development as a young prairie socialist. As a young man he observed what he saw as an analogy to the Rebellions (albeit without the shedding of blood), and then was socialized into a democratic socialist academic perspective by Frank A. Underhill.

Clark's affiliation with the prairie farmers' revolt in the 1920s and 1930s—the highpoints in the rebellion of the agrarian petite bourgeoisie (Conway 1983a; Laycock 1990) against extinction as a result of the changes wrought by industrial capitalism—was followed by post-graduate study at Toronto where he quickly came under the influence not of Chester Martin, but Frank H. Underhill. Underhill was born in Ontario in 1889 and educated at the University of Toronto and at Oxford. He taught at the University of Saskatchewan in 1914-15 and after the First World War until 1927, at which point he moved to the University of Toronto. He quickly became seized with enthusiasm for the various movements of the agrarian petite bourgeoisie. He became a prolific supporter of and writer for the *Canadian Forum* and a founder of the League for Social Reconstruction, and he "wrote the first draft of the Regina Manifesto, the party platform of the CCF" (Storey 1967, 809). Underhill became known for his views on the political participation of academics. "He opposed the concept of academic detachment from political problems as an evasion of responsibility pointing out that political involvement is part of the tradition of the British intellectual" (ibid.).

In an academic sense, Underhill had become a devotee of a "North American school of interpretation" which, basing itself on the work of the American historian F.J. Turner, "emphasized the vertical connections north and south." The interpretation held that "Canadian history has shown the development not of a British but of a North American society" especially "in the matter of class distinction and in much of the spirit and practice of political democracy, religion, and education" (Kilbourn 1965, 501). Members of the school tended to compare the openness of the American class system to the more closed nature of the Canada system.

Underhill was at the University of Saskatchewan during the strongest point of the agrarian movement. Norman Penlington writes: "He was much moved by observing western democracy in action—the Progressive party, the grain pools, and the protests against eastern manufacture and finance" (1971, xi). As Berger comments, Underhill "was caught up in the passion of Western protest . . . " (1976, 59). As indicated above, Underhill was not one to divorce scholarship from contemporary life and politics. His first professional paper on Canadian history, published in 1927, was a discussion of the agrarian composition and radical ideas of the Grit movement (political reformers) of the 1850s and 1860s in Upper Canada. The parallel to the agrarian crisis of the 1920s was made quite explicit, "But out in the territory of the Red and Saskatchewan, the clear Grit movement has come to life again in a fresh incarnation, and the farmers of the prairies are unconsciously reviving many of the ideas for which the farmers of what was then western Canada strove two generations ago. With that Upper Canada which read the Globe and voted Grit we of the modern West have a natural affinity. It is our spiritual home" (1960, 67).

It is interesting to note that Underhill recants his former position somewhat in his introduction to this essay when it was reprinted in *In Search of Canadian Liberalism* (1960): "It was written while I was a professor in Saskatchewan and therefore particularly apt to see the parallels between agrarian movements in Upper Canada in the 1860s and agrarian movements in the prairies in the 1920s. It rather overemphasized the agrarian aspect of Grittism; and I modified this view somewhat by the time of my address in 1946 to the CHA (Canadian Historical Association) on the Canadian liberal tradition" (1960, 43). However, by the late 1940s academic criticisms of the frontier perspective and of the agrarian nature of the Clear Grits were on the horizon. Such a one was J.M.S. Careless's article, "The Toronto Globe and Agrarian Radicalism, 1850-1867" (1948) which tried to refute Underhill's frontierist interpretation. By the 1950s Underhill had become a supporter of the Liberal Party and in 1960 he received a Governor-General's award in non-fiction for *In Search of Canadian Liberalism*.

At any rate, it was the early "frontier socialist" Underhill who became an important mentor of S.D. Clark. In the 1930s both men were democratic socialists involved with the CCF and with other social democratic movements; both men were adherents of F.J. Turner's frontierism and agreed on its relevance to Canada; both men were sympathetic to a wide use of class analysis; both men were suspicious of the impact of British institutions on Canadian society; both men tended to rebel against the constitutionalist perspective of such historians as G.M. Wrong and Chester Martin; and both men looked instead to the socio-economic underpinnings of social change.

Although Underhill did later retreat from frontierism, Clark remained an adherent throughout this period. Even as late as 1959, he was to write, "The American revolution in Canada had not yet by 1850 come to an end. It had still perhaps not come to an end by 1935 when the people of Alberta marched to the polls and voted to make their province a sovereign state in the management of monetary affairs . . . the forces underlying the Social Credit uprising in Alberta were not vastly different from the forces underlying the Riel rebellion on the North Saskatchewan in 1885, and neither of these uprisings differed in any fundamental way from the uprisings in Lower and Upper Canada in 1837" (1959, 502-503).

Conclusion

On the basis of the relativistic nature of knowledge production identified by the sociology of knowledge and by certain historical traditions, it seems that no detached positivistic account of knowledge production alone could explain Clark's decision to adopt a favourable rather than a negative interpretation of the 1837 Rebellions. Rather, his interpretation was bound up with his biographical development as a farm boy from the western prairies during a comparable period of unrest in the 1920s and 1930s, with the influence of William Irvine, William Wise Wood and the CCF and with his academic network which included such a prominent democratic socialist and frontierist historian as F.H. Underhill.

Other interpretations of the Rebellions which do not see them in so positive a light—such as those produced by Aileen Dunham and Chester Martin among others—reveal the marked divergence of negative and positive views of the Rebellions. But such variance goes back a very long way and has survived the transition from filiopietistic to more "scientific" history. It is likely no "refutation" of either view is possible except on very delimited matters, thus underscoring the view that Clark had academic justification in whichever interpretation he chose to adopt.

It is now recognized by the sociology of knowledge that knowledge is *not* produced by heroic individuals working alone simply responding to facts, but emerges from within established paradigms buttressed by practical support mechanisms (Kuhn 1962). The career of S.D. Clark clearly exemplifies that this is so.

Chapter Four

John Porter and the 'Matthew Effect': Canadian Development and 'The Pattern Variables'

The Matthew Effect in scientific communication, according to Robert K. Merton, is the process by which "eminent scientists get disproportionately great credit for their contributions to science" (Merton 1968, 57). The name of this phenomenon comes from the Christian New Testament of St. Matthew in which Jesus says, "For unto every one that hath shall be given, and he shall have abundance; but from him that hath not shall be taken away even that which he hath" (cited in Merton 1968, 58).

Some instances of this effect cited by Merton include the attribution of primary credit for co-authored papers to a better known scientist even when this is not merited, and the positive evaluation of an author's previous research due to her or his later fame (1973, 444). Another illustration of the Matthew Effect comes in reference to independent multiple discoveries when nearly the same ideas or findings are separately communicated by a "scientist of great repute and by one not yet widely known" (ibid.). In such cases the already known author will get the lion's share of the credit. Because of the "information explosion" only a small percentage of journal articles are actually read by any one scientist in any particular field (half of one percent in chemistry). However, one study cited by Merton found that between 15 and 23 percent of "the psychologist-readers' behaviours in selecting articles were based on the identity of the authors" (1968, 59).

It can be argued that John Porter's fame has been elevated beyond the point where such fame is actually merited because of the Matthew Effect. One corollary of the Matthew Effect is to blunt criticism which would be directed at lesser known authors. Almost anything that a famous author says will be taken to be of interest by a scientific community, even if it is not related to the author's specialty (for example the publicity received by Nobel laureate John Polanyi on nuclear disarmament); and if the celebrated scientist's comments *are* related to his or her own field, then this comment is taken as even more germane (Clarkson 1985, 341).

I doubt that anyone would debate the point that much of John Porter's fame has come about because of his writing on the nature of the Canadian economic and political elites. His material is modern-oriented (unlike the work of S.D. Clark) and was instantly perceived as relevant to discussions on power in contemporary Canada. As Dennis Olsen suggests, "Here at home he became the most widely read and cited English-speaking sociologist both within the university and without" (1981, 609).

In the United States Irving Louis Horowitz commences his important review in the *American Sociological Review* with the laudatory comments, "Only the informal prohibition on adjectival excess prevents me from beginning the review of Porter's book with raves. Suffice it to say, this is *the* sociological study of present-day Canada . . . ." (1966, cited in Heap 1974, 5). The complimentary review in the American Sociological Association's flagship publication was reinforced by Porter's selection as the 1966 MacIver Award recipient. His MacIver address was subsequently published by the *ASR* (Porter 1968, reprinted in Porter 1979).

Edwin R. Black points out that, "With more than seventy thousand copies sold since 1965, *The Vertical Mosaic* must be the runaway best seller of Canadian social science. Those sales are surely deserved, for John Porter's book must be accounted the single most influential Canadian book published since the second world war" (1974, 640). As Gad Horowitz observes, *The Vertical Mosaic* received publicity far beyond the normal academic volume: "The Canadian public has been introduced to Porter's study primarily through reviews which have appeared in a number of newspapers, in *Time* magazine, and on the CBC" (1965, in Heap 1974, 11).

In addition, I would suggest that the trend in Canadian sociology after 1970 toward a conflict-oriented, even neo-Marxist approach, has tended to strengthen Porter's reputation for reasons which are not strictly related to the merits of his work. One factor is identified by Martin Robin, better known as a labour historian, but who, in fact, received a PhD from the department of sociology at the University of Toronto in 1966 (Helmes-Hayes 1968, 43). Robin castigates Canadian social scientists for having "sorely neglected . . . . Canada's class system and power structure" in favour of "probing the anatomy of formal political institutions" (1966, in Heap 1974, 1). Porter, he suggests, provides "an admirable antidote to the formalistic obsessions of Canadian academicians" (ibid., 11).

It would be miserly not to recognize the manifold merits of Porter's work and its influence on Canadian sociology. However, from the perspective of modern critical sociology, John Porter was heavily influenced at points in his work by structural-functionalism of the sort developed by Talcott Parsons, R.K. Merton, S.M. Lipset and others. Some subjects discussed by Porter bear the effects of this influence in a way that seems quite regrettable and, due to the Matthew Effect, these parts of Porter's work may be taken more seriously than they deserve to be. The constant citation of Porter's work on the Anglican church is a case in point (almost every sociologist mentioning

Canadian Anglicanism cites this sadly deficient portion of his work and usually in a positive or least neutral manner) and is proof that the Matthew Effect is at work. Other areas of Porter's work which need to be criticized as deficient due to his poor integration of a structural functionalist approach are his writings on Canadian and Québec socioeconomic backwardness (*vis-a-vis* the United States).

As Harvey Rich suggests, *The Vertical Mosaic* "enjoyed a spectacularly successful career" and there has been a tendency to cite it as "*the* authoritative reference" to a wide number of fields (1976, 15). Indeed, one would have to agree with Rich that this book, due to the Matthew Effect no doubt, has had "until recently a near-immunity from criticism and [a] ritualistic instead of critical use . . . of the data in it" and that such unreflective appreciation has been "a disservice to the author" as well as to students and citizens "who rely on social scientists to provide critical scrutiny and rejection or modification of unfounded interpretations and conclusions" (ibid.). This was true during the 1960s and much of the 1970s, but is much less true of the 1980s. A fair measure of this criticism of the 1980s can be found in Brym (1986) and Brym with Fox (1989). An earlier critique is made by Heap (1974, 89-163).

The aim of this chapter is not to destroy Porter's reputation—which will last regardless of assaults—or to destroy structural functionalism. My perspective is that science and social science and academic study in general, are areas of critical debate and exchange. Much in Porter will survive and certainly his exercise of the sociological imagination will remain to emulate. Unlike many Marxist sociologists, I would suggest there is much in an empirically-based structural functionalism which is of merit (for example, the work of much but not all of Durkheim and Merton); my critical comments on this point are aimed rather specifically at the structural functional writing related to modernization.

Anglicanism and John Porter

In *The Vertical Mosaic*, Porter points out that 52 of 57 Roman Catholic bishops were Canadian born as opposed to 10 of 26 Anglican bishops in 1952. Porter specifically emphasizes this as a problem for the Anglican Church in his statement that "Catholic bishops know their communities through having grown up in them and are, therefore, able to articulate a Catholic view about Canada which has meaning for the Catholic population of Canada." About Anglican bishops, Porter comments, "It is unlikely that a group such as the Anglican hierarchy, which recruits so heavily from those born and brought up outside the country, can articulate a native ideology for Canada. No such problem exists for the Catholic hierarchy" (1965, 515).

Porter points to two particular bishops to exemplify the sorts of problems Canadian Anglicanism might be experiencing. Then Bishop of Montréal, K.

Maguire, consecrated to his see in 1962, "had been in Canada less than two years before his election." The other example cited is the Most Reverend Philip Carrington, "a former archbishop of Québec [who] served in Canada for thirty-three years and in 1960 returned to live in England, his 'native land' after retirement." Although the data do not indicate that these are significant trends, Porter's selective citation of Maguire provides a portrait of the parachute Anglican bishop, elected to office in Canada with little Canadian experience, and unlikely to remain in the country with little in the way of real roots or attachment to this country. One immediate criticism of Porter's discussion of Maguire is that he had spent five years in Canada divided over two periods of two and three years interrupted by eight years back in his native Ireland.

Archbishop Carrington, also maligned by Porter as the archtype of the foreign parachute bishop, published one of the relatively few general works on *The Anglican Church in Canada* (1963), a work which is still of value. In addition, Carrington was far from being the normal "English" bishop. Of his thirty-five years before his move to Canada in 1927, twenty were spent in New Zealand and Australia and fifteen in England (Cuttell 1988, 161). After his retirement to England in 1960, Carrington returned to Canada as a Professor of Theology from 1962-1964 (ibid., 163) at St. John's College, Winnipeg.

Because of Porter's general acclaim and perhaps because of the underdeveloped state of the sociology of religion in Canada, many sociologists were quick to rely on Porter's view on Anglicanism in Canada. Well-known sociologists such Crysdale and Montminy (1974, 69), Westhues (1976, 299), Harry H. Hiller (1976, 381), Ogmundson (1980, 7), Mol (1985, 217-218) and Bibby (1987, 286) all draw on Porter's portrait of a Canadian episcopate with little in the way of Canadian roots. This reliance ranges from rather brief citations to brief descriptive summaries of his conclusions.

I have several criticisms of both Porter's methodologies and conceptualizations. Firstly, by focusing on the instances of Maguire and Carrington, Porter is guilty of selective citation as very few Anglican bishops of non-Canadian background, at least after 1900, were "parachutes" with little Canadian experience and very few retired to Britain, or anywhere else but Canada. For example, during the period of 1902-1927, of the foreign-born Anglican bishops in Canada, 67 percent had become priests while in Canada, (normally at about age twenty-three). The comparable figure for 1928-1961 was 78 percent (Nock 1981, 96). Between 1902 and 1975, of sixty-three foreign-born bishops only five (or 8 percent) had spent less than seven years in Canada before receiving a mitre (Nock 1981, 89). One of these, of course, was Bishop Maguire with his five years here. At an earlier period (1787-1901) when the church was in its infancy in many areas, the comparable figure had been 43 percent, but as Canada's population matured and as election by Canadian synods became the norm after 1857, the "parachute bishop" became close to being an endangered species. As far as the retirement or death of bishops was concerned, of all the bishops who suffered one or the other termination to their career *only one* of thirty-five (3 percent) did so outside of Canada—Archbishop Carrington himself (Nock 1979, 54; 1981, 89).

If one simply considers the birthplace of Anglican bishops and ignores the general pattern of the life long immigrant there is more to the assertion of the predominance of British birth. Between 1867 and 1901, 72 percent of Canadian bishops were British by birth. The comparable figures for 1902 to 1927 were 59 percent and for 1928 to 1949, 49 percent. However in 1955, the Church of England in Canada changed its name to the Anglican Church of Canada, and this seemed to act as a symbol as the large majority of Anglican bishops since have been Canadian born (Nock 1981, 97). In the period of October 1955 (when the name was changed) to 1961, 81 percent of new bishops were Canadian born, the remainder being British.

Porter is quick enough to cite the election of Irish-born Bishop Maguire in 1962, but he does not observe the rapid and dramatic change to Canadian-born bishops. Part of the problem is methodological: by taking the single year of 1952, Porter lumps together all bishops currently still in office no matter when they were consecrated. My data all compare and contrast the character-istics of bishops consecrated between certain specific time periods. Retire-ment has only recently become a norm for bishops, thus Porter compares bishops elected several decades previously to those just installed (Nock 1981, 88). Since Porter's data all centre on the year 1952, he does not recognize the rapid Canadianization of bishops which took place *after* 1954.

However my underlying point in this analysis is that John Porter was likely to exaggerate and even produce misleading and erroneous statements about Canadian Anglicanism because it fit in with his functionalist theory of modernization, a theory characteristic of the 1950s and 1960s. This theory suggests that modernization (almost invariably a good thing to sociologists of that period) is most likely when a nation or a region adopts the set of values extracted from Talcott Parson's pattern variables which were conducive to modernity—egalitarianism, achievement, universalism, specificity, affective neutrality and self-orientation. Such a swing to modernity was strongest in Western countries such as the United States which had been liberal societies uninfluenced by a feudal or aristocratic past. Britain, however, had been strongly influenced by such a past and the Church of England which was part of the English establishment, had the right to seat twenty-six bishops in the House of Lords and was a traditional supporter and avenue of talent for the landed classes. Thus to John Porter, it was natural to assume that the Church of England would continue to act as a conservative and even reactionary influence in the new land. The fact that certain facets of Canadian history were capable of such an interpretation (such as the fight over the Clergy Reserves up until 1854[1]) made it all the more possible to dovetail such a view with the theories of modernization being developed by Parsons, Lipset, Bellah and other structural-functionalist theorists. Porter highlights what may be dubbed the "Anglican transplantation" argument when he writes "It may be that Anglican leaders see themselves as representing an eternal link with Great Britain, Canterbury, and the Crown" (1965, 515). A more recent upholder of this argument is Roger O'Toole who ironically may be sustaining rather than shattering sociological myths. He writes,

> In English Canada, the monopolistic attempt of Anglicanism to impose itself as a national church was thwarted by the resistance of nonconformity led by such spokesmen as Egerton Ryerson. The failure of establishmentarianism came too late, however, to prevent it infusing some pungent ingredients into the political atmosphere, particularly in Upper Canada. Its proclamation that the Anglo-Saxon burden of Empire, monarchy, aristocracy, and British constitutionalism were part of a sacred scenario and, by the same token, its condemnation of mass democracy, egalitarianism, republicanism and revolution as the work of the devil left an indelible mark on English-Canadian political life. It appears reasonable to suppose that the conservative counter-revolutionary, "law-and-order" identity which some observers detect and perceive as characteristically and distinctively English-Canadian, is at least in some measure, the legacy of Bishop Strachan and his fellow Churchmen (1984, 80).

Before leaving Anglicanism, I would like to underline that Porter failed to appreciate important differences between Canadian Anglicanism and English Anglicanism. The first of these is the Canadian system of *election* of bishops by synods composed of both clerical and lay delegates. This system was first introduced in 1857 in the diocese of Huron, and wherever the population was settled and substantial (with the important exception of Newfoundland which, of course, was not part of Canada) it soon came to be adopted as the main selection mechanism. However the innovation of synods, with its mix of episcopal, clerical *and* lay delegates, had been pioneered by Bishop Strachan who in 1851 had invited the laity to attend his visitation which in the words of William Westfall, "became in effect the first diocesan synod" (1989, 113). The second diocesan conference in 1853 declared itself a synod and assumed the power to deal with the affairs of the church. Westfall notes, "It was the first synod with lay delegates held in the British Empire" (ibid., 114).

This move toward diocesan synods with power to elect bishops, constitutional self-government, and its mix of lay and clerical delegates cast Bishop Strachan into the role of clerical pioneer and rebel. As Westfall notes, "In fact Strachan had moved before he had the clear authority to initiate such reforms" (ibid.). Strachan had solicited legal opinions about the legality of convening synods only to be told of prohibitions against clerical convocations. The British government was "wary of granting" requests for the power to convene synods "primarily because of its implications for the church in Britain" (ibid.). In effect Strachan went ahead anyway and cut through a sea of red tape and ambiguity. Strachan had entertained thoughts of this nature since as far back as 1836 (Roper 1988, 261). Roper comments, "It is surely an in indication of Strachan's force of character and perception of changing realities that in 1853 he turned his next visitation into a synod, even though no legal authority existed to enable this to be done. The great Tory, like many Tories before and since, was willing to undertake a revolutionary act when circumstances demanded it" (ibid., 262). It was perhaps ironic, but increasingly typical in Canada, that Strachan "despite his life-long antipathy towards the American Republic, [had] looked south for the idea of diocesan synods" (ibid., 261).

The upshot of these changes was the *first elected* bishop, not just in Canada but in the British Empire when the diocese of Huron was carved out of southwestern Ontario. Despite Strachan's own hand being behind these changes, matters did not go his own way. His chosen candidate (Archdeacon A.N. Bethune, later second Bishop of Toronto), was ignored in favour of Benjamin Cronyn. Roper comments, "The tone of the battle in the press showed conclusively that the Church of England in Canada had definitively entered the brawling world of North American democracy" (ibid., 265). In contrast, in England the *appointment* of bishops (nominally by the Crown) continues. Politically, the adoption of electoral synods represented a move to democracy as opposed to hierarchy. One immediate consequence was the virtual elimination of parachute bishops wherever electoral synods were the basis for selection, whereas the majority of Crown-appointed bishops in Canada and Newfoundland between 1787 and 1937 continued to be "parachutes" as opposed to career immigrants (Nock 1981, 95).

The minority status of Anglicans in Canada meant a need for the church to depend upon the voluntary offerings of its members; diocesan synods insured that no excessive alienation developed between followers and leaders and that a more democratic ethos developed in Canadian Anglicanism. It must be remembered that in England the Church is established as an ally of the state and of the Crown. Between 1830 and 1850 it became clear that there would be no established Anglicanism in Canada. This meant that Anglicanism "would be a denomination like any other" and would change "from a church supported by the state to one in which support came from below" (Roper

1988, 262). Depending on offerings was difficult partly because of "the poverty in congregations in the Maritimes and the Canadas," but also because the church's previous status as an established church had "reduced incentive for local giving" (ibid.).

Not only was there a problem in getting congregations to donate enough, but on the clerical (and episcopal) side there was apprehension that "voluntarism" (meaning the system of self-support by congregations and parishioners) "would weaken the hierarchical principle that was at the heart of the estab-lishment system. Once the clergy were paid by their parishioners, they became the prisoner of local interests and relied upon the very people over whom they were supposed to exercise spiritual guidance" (Westfall 1989, 100). Upholders of traditional Anglicanism rejected the individualistic mar-ket-oriented idea that people should choose their own religion or their own clergy. They held the view that "the depravity of human nature made people very poor judges of their own religious needs" (ibid., 101).

Despite such problems and fears, the church did move quickly to make itself less reliant on external sources of support. "Bishop Strachan, only two years after his appointment as First Bishop of Toronto, declared that the period has therefore arrived . . . when the parishes and congregations must be appealed to on the necessity of contributing towards the support of their respective ministers. And I trust there will be no backwardness in answering such an appeal" (ibid., 105).

In short, Canadian Anglicanism was not simply a transplant of an hierar-chical British church, but had been influenced by its own unique Canadian environment which included an incorporation of a number of democratic tendencies. A latter-day example of this distinctiveness from the English church has been the Canadian church's significantly earlier movement on the issue of the ordination of women. Women have been ordained in Canada since 1974, but only in 1992 was a decision to proceed to women's ordination made in England and it will be several more years before the first such ordination occurs.

US—Canada Comparisons

In his essay, "Canadian Character in the Twentieth Century," Porter pursues an interesting and somewhat unusual thesis—that English and French Cana-dians despite linguistic, historical, cultural and religious differences are rather similar. This similarity lies in their common "conservativism, traditionalism, religiosity, authoritarianism, and elitist values" (1979, 100). He wonders (surely answered affirmatively in his own mind) "if, after all, there is not a single culture in Canada in which the core values are conservative" with only subcultural variation between the English and French. It seems to Porter that the relative equilibrium between French and English in Canada rests on "a mutual defence of these cultural elements in North America . . . " (ibid.).

Porter looks with favour on "the egalitarian model of the United States." He suggests that "modern industrial societies" are characterized by a readiness for change "in the interests of adaptability." Such change is normally greeted with more readiness among elites than among the mass of the population. However in Canada, resistance to such necessary change "characterizes elites as well as the mass of the population and pervades most of its institutions to a greater degree than in the United States," and he muses whether this pursuit of conservatism will continue or not after the "centenary year" of 1967 (ibid., 100).

In drawing such a portrait, Porter relies on the well-developed analysis of such sociologists as S.D. Clark, Dennis Wrong, Kaspar Naegele and S.M. Lipset (Porter 1979, 99). Porter draws on Lipset's theme of the counter-revolutionary background to Canadian history and contrasts "the strong egalitarianism of the United States" with Canadians who are "authoritarian, oriented to tradition, hierarchy and elitism in the sense of showing deference to those in high status" (ibid.). Porter concludes that, "It would be difficult to disagree with Lipset" and cites as an example Canada's comparative neglect of education. He suggested that "industrialization is in, but not of Canada" and that "the values necessary to support industrialization are not as strong in Canada as in the United States" and that "egalitarian values . . . are essential to high levels of industrialization" (ibid.).

Of the four authors mentioned by Porter as influencing his own view, three were products of structural functionalism. S.M. Lipset pursued his graduate education at Columbia University and was influenced strongly by Robert K. Merton (Lipset 1969, 174). According to Lipset, his increasing concern with stability as well as change meant "that theorists such as Emile Durkheim, Alexis de Tocqueville, and Talcott Parsons took on much more importance in my work then they had originally" (ibid., 173). As he began to develop comparisons of social development, Lipset concluded that "the Parsonian pattern variables formed the most useful set of classifications for such comparative analysis" (ibid., 163). Lipset became known in Canada because of his research on the CCF, his residence in Saskatchewan and his short period as a lecturer at the University of Toronto, from 1946 to 1948 (Helmes- Hayes 1988, 59).

Kasper Naegele was a Parsons PhD (Mullins 197, 51) but also became a scholarly collaborator and was a co-editor along with Parsons, Edward Shils and Jesse R. Pitts of the large two-volume *Theories in Society* (1961). He came to Canada from Harvard University and taught at the University of British Columbia until his death. Talcott Parsons dedicated *Sociological Theory and Modern Society* (1967) to Naegele's memory as did John Porter with *The Vertical Mosaic*. In his dedication, Parsons describes Naegele as a "perceptive observer, imaginative theorist, beloved friend to very many." Porter memorializes Naegele as one "whose contributions to Canada and to the understanding of Canadian society will be greatly missed" (1965, v).

Dennis Wrong was Canadian, but received his PhD in 1956 from Columbia and thereafter remained in the United States, particularly at New York University (Mullins 1973, 56-57). He spent the academic year of 1955-56 as a lecturer at the University of Toronto (Helmes-Hayes 1988, 60).

It is little wonder that this school of interpretation (dubbed "cultural theory" by R.J. Brym [1986, 19]) became predominant in the 1950s and 1960s. S.D. Clark had been known for several decades as the dean of English Canadian sociology and was a very high profile sociologist at the prestigious University of Toronto (and was a full Professor from 1953). He was made the first Chairman (as the position was then called) of the department of sociology when the department was created in 1963 (and remained so until 1969) and had been a president of the prestigious Royal Society of Canada. John Porter was at a newer and lesser known university, but his own research had the advantage of being more immediately and more obviously relevant to understanding Canadian society, and it was more obviously sociology than Clark's work. Particularly with *The Vertical Mosaic*, Porter became close to being a celebrity in his own country and certainly became recognized as sociology's leading star in Canada. His eminence was confirmed in the minds of Canadians and Americans when he was awarded the MacIver prize in 1967. A recent study of four introductory textbooks published by Canadian sociologists in the 1980s indicates John Porter is still the most cited Canadian sociologist (Saram 1986, 3).

By the 1960s S.M. Lipset had become probably the third most cited sociologist in American sociology textbooks, and this pattern lasted into the 1970s (Wells 1979, 434). His ranking was just after Parsons and Merton. Of course, both Wrong and Naegele also became well known, although not quite to the same extent as Clark, Porter, and Lipset.

Regarding the trio mentioned above, it must be added that their interpretation easily fitted into the prevailing paradigm of structural functionalism, emphasizing as it did a relative celebration of the western civilizational matrix and, methodologically, a relative emphasis on the importance of homogeneous values. Thus the growing fame of several individual scholars was buttressed by their acceptance of a currently predominant paradigm. In addition, there were a number of common personal links—Wrong had received his BA in 1945 at Toronto when Clark was teaching there, and Clark taught at the University of Toronto when Lipset came as a young Lecturer in 1946-48. Although Clark and Porter had not been trained at the main seats of functionalism, Lipset, Wrong and Naegele had. As Brym comments, "An entire study in the sociology of knowledge could be written about the social linkages between, and common influences on, most of these men . . . " (1986, 13).

Underdevelopment in Québec

One of the more deep-seated effects of functionalism on Porter is evident in his accounting for the socioeconomic backwardness in Québec and among French Canadians. Structural functionalism developed a comprehensive approach to modernization based on Parson's "pattern variables." These variables are a number of matched comparative ideal type values which can be used for measuring the degree of modernity a nation has attained. A discussion of the pattern variables in relation to theories of modernization may be found in Lipset's *The First New Nation* (1963, 241-43). Lipset defines achievement-ascription as follows:

> a society's value system may emphasize individual ability or performance or it may emphasize ascribed or inherited qualities (such as race or high birth) in judging individuals and placing them in various roles. According to the universalism-particularism distinction, it may emphasize that all people shall be treated according to the same standard (e.g. equality before the law), or that individuals shall be treated differently according to their personal qualities or their particular membership in a class or group, Specificity- diffuseness refers to the difference between treating individuals in terms of the specific positions which they happen to occupy, rather than diffusely as individual members of the collectivity (Lipset 1963, 240).

Later on Lipset defines collectivity-orientation as "the extent to which values emphasize that a collectivity has a claim on the individual units within it to conform to the defined interests of the larger group, as contrasted to a stress on actions predominantly reflecting the perceived needs of the units (ibid., 309).

It was assumed by structural functionalists that most nations or regions had more or less complete control over which values they adopted, that early experiences at certain formative periods were crucial (in the instance of the United States the Puritan experiment and the American Revolution (ibid., 119-120), that once values were established they changed slowly (ibid., 17), and that rather than being at the mercy of economic and political institutions, these values had the power to shape economic and political institutions (ibid., 140). Wherever a country or region was seen to be socioeconomically backward, it was deemed to be because of inappropriate values. Even where a country became strong without the advantage of a Protestant and Calvinist background, as in Japan, it was because of a functional substitute for such values (Bellah 1957; Bellah 1964).

While Porter was involved in researching and writing *The Vertical*

Mosaic in the 1940s and 1950s, a school of historians at the Université de Montréal was developing which concentrated on the negative impact of the British Conquest on the subsequent development of French Canada. These historians—Guy Frégault, Maurice Séguin, and Michel Brunet—became among the most successful and celebrated in Québec, and in Canada. Although their work was controversial and remains so, and although their central thesis has been contested by other Québec historians (notably those trained at or teaching at Laval), one would have expected that their views would cause Porter either to reconsider his views or at least to move him to counter such interpretations (see Brunet 1964; Cook 1966, 126-42; Cook 1971, 129-40).

It should be pointed out that Brunet's important book of 1964, *La Présence Anglaise et les Canadiens* is largely a republication of previous essays bearing on the effects of the Conquest. Most were published in the 1950s and thus should have been accessible to Porter. An early volume of Brunet's writing is *Canadians et Canadiens* (1954). In one of the articles, "Problèmes Contemporains de la Société Canadienne-Française," Brunet expresses in embryo his thesis of the devastation of the Conquest (109-111).

Thus work of the Montréal School appeared early enough for Porter to use in *The Vertical Mosaic*, but Séguin, Frégault and Brunet are not cited or quoted in the text. Two factors as to why this was so come to mind. Was this an instance where disciplinary boundaries played an unfortunate role? After all, most of us tend to read primarily within our own disciplinary boundaries even if we are aware of cross disciplinary developments. Secondly, could this have been an instance of "the two solitudes" between the two linguistic and academic worlds? For example, there are five citations to S.D. Clark's work but none of J.C. Falardeau's who had become the first well-established university sociologist in French Canada, and none of Léon Gérin's who was a Québec sociologist before its university institutionalization.

Porter's failure to learn French may also have been an impeding factor. Marion Porter informs us that John Porter did not know French and that "his failure" to master French was one of the "disappointments" of his later years (M. Porter 1988, 5). She points out that he did master Italian during the Second World War and had thought he could do the same with French. She writes, "it is one thing to be able to ask a few questions and another to engage in an intellectual discussion" but that he never had the time or drive to learn French adequately (ibid.).

At any rate, John Porter advocates an interpretation fully compatible with functionalism's stress on the autonomous role of values and ideologies. Porter rejects the Montréal School indirectly and a mass of sociological writing when he states, "In view of the power of French Canadians within some systems of power it is difficult to accept the theory of British exploitation" (1965, 93). Instead he points to the "outstanding example of institutional failure" provided by the educational system (ibid., 92), emphasizes that French-Canadian education "was never geared to the provision of industrial skills at the managerial or technical level" (ibid.), and states that "because of its Catholic values it did not experience that cultural coalescing of Protestant dogma and commercial values that Max Weber wrote about in his celebrated work, *The Protestant Ethic and the Spirit of Capitalism*" (ibid., 95).

As an interpretation, this one actually seems a *regression* from that provided by University of Chicago exemplar, E.C. Hughes in *French Canada in Transition*, published a generation earlier in 1943. Although Hughes espouses some aspects of a cultural explanation (1943, 61), he pays very considerable attention to the role of ethnic stereotypes and to the custom of mentoring between culturally homogeneous people—to put it differently, he looks at the roles that prejudice and discrimination played (ibid., 51-58, 62). In his paper "Images of Inequality in Early Canadian Sociology, 1900-1965," Richard Helmes-Hayes suggests that Hughes "contributed . . . to the move-ment away from 'culturalist' explanations of social structure and change in Québec . . . " (1986, 18). Thus it seems reasonable to conclude that Porter failed to take into account such different interpretations as those provided by Hughes and the Montréal School because he had became too dependent on functionalism.

Conclusion

Perhaps I can end this chapter by attempting to explain why Porter had become so dependent on functionalism, and then by returning to a few comments on the Matthew Effect. I do *not* assert that Porter was a functional-ist in the committed sense of Parsons, Lipset, Merton, Levy or other consis-tent theoretical developers of that tradition. My own reading of Porter is, in fact, that he was not theoretically committed in any systematic way. Porter saw himself as an empirical researcher for whom getting down to the raw data was of primary importance. He leaned toward the empiricist view that facts would speak for themselves if only the facts were discovered. Thus, I feel that Porter was something of a theoretical chameleon. In the words of Irving Louis Horowitz, "Mr. Porter takes his theory where he can find it: from Marx, Weber, Mills, Warner, Parsons" (1966, cited in Heap 1974, 5). He slaved mightily to discover "facts" and then gave less than sufficient consideration to what the facts might mean. As a consequence, he tended to be influenced by whatever the prevailing theoretical winds might be. In the 1950s and 1960s Porter was a functionalist. In the 1970s, he started to incorporate more affection for conflict interpretations (Clement 1980, 110; Marion Porter 1981, 633). I doubt this would have worried Porter given his emphasis on empirical research.

This interpretation of Porter is reinforced by his "foreword" to Wallace

Clement's *The Canadian Corporate Elite* (1975), a work which was first written as an MA thesis under Porter's direction and was intended, at least in part, as a data update one generation after for the economic elite. In this foreword, Porter writes, "I have never been dogmatic about the theories and frameworks by which we seek to give order to the facts that emerge from our research . . . the facts often speak for themselves regardless of the framework within which they are presented" (1975, x). Porter's empiricist and positivistic orientation is also revealed in his comment, "Unless there is some slugging after facts, theoretical debates are abstract and hollow whether the schoolmen who engage in them are medieval or contemporary" (ibid.). Wallace Clement adds to this interpretation of Porter when he points out that "it was [Porter's] judgement that the priority was empirical rather than theoretical" and that he relied on an "'eclectic' use of theory" (Clement 1980, 99). Similar points are echoed by John R. Hofley who suggests that Porter was "impatient with theoretical arguments" and that he "always wanted to move on to the 'facts' . . . ." (1981, 600).

I hope I will evade being labelled a "schoolman" but I would argue that Porter gave too little shrift to theory in his slogging after facts. Ironically, however, it is my own fear (confirmed by the constant citation of Porter's inept studies on Anglicanism) that what may represent his own worst research, using the least adequate formulations of functionalist modernization theory, will continue to be cited as standard sociological writing on the Anglican Church of Canada when, in fact, it deserves to be forgotten. In his 1968 article on the Matthew Effect, R.K. Merton tended to stress its positive functions (see also Merton 1973, 447-448) in bringing to notice work which might otherwise be ignored if signed by or attributed to an unknown. However the Matthew Effect has functions which are less fortifying—it legitimates research which is distinctly second drawer in quality but which is rendered quotable because of implicit assumptions made by readers of sociology about the quality of a distinguished person's entire corpus of work.

Note

[1] The clergy Reserves were lands in Ontario (or Upper Canada as it was then) set aside for the maintenance of the Protestant religion between 1791 and 1854. Up to one-seventh of all Crown land was so set apart. Until near the end of this period "Protestant" was interpreted to mean Church of England.

Chapter Five

The Social Construction of Reputation in Anglo-Canadian Sociology

One of the earliest authors to produce a social account of the production of knowledge was the doctor-scientist Ludwik Fleck in his *Genesis and Development of a Scientific Fact* (1935; reprinted in 1979). Published in the midst of the traumatic events of the 1930s and printed in Switzerland, its substantive theme was a history of how syphilis has been conceived and dealt with in succeeding eras of western society.

The book was almost ignored in the 1930s, but was revised in 1979 by Thomas Kuhn and Robert Merton because of its theory which emphasized the communal nature of knowledge. Fleck asserts that knowledge is "the most socially-conditioned activity of men and knowledge is the paramount social creation" (1979, 42). Such social factors as propaganda, imitation, authority, rivalry, solidarity, enmity and friendship influence the production of knowledge and Fleck deemed as trivial "every epistemological theory . . . that does not take this sociological dependence of all cognition into account in a fundamental and detailed manner" (ibid., 43). Fleck rejected positivist theorists who consider social dependence in knowledge as an evil to be overcome as "without such social conditioning no cognition is even possible" (ibid.).

Why was the book ignored? Perhaps because it was misinterpreted as mainly dealing with syphilis instead of as a general contribution to epistemology. Also, surely political and military events weighed on the mind in the Europe of the later 1930s, rather than epistemology.

This chapter analyzes the structure of citations in Robert J. Brym's (with Bonnie J. Fox) volume *From Culture to Power: The Sociology of English Canada* (1989). My operating hypothesis is that the choice of citations is more than just a reflex reaction to the accumulated literature and reflects deep-seated social influences on the production of knowledge. I particularly wish to emphasize the issues of regionalism, personal networks, and graduate school.

The choice of regionalism as an element for analysis would seem obvious in Canada where it is a deep-seated part of the population's identity. Regionalism is discussed as an important factor in the production of sociology by Straus and Radel (1969). Crane (1967) discusses the importance of doctoral training and graduate school in advancing personal networks. Nicholas Mullins (1973) discusses more comprehensively the influence of networks in the construction of sociological paradigms. Berkowitz suggests that there is "strong theoretical and empirical cause to believe that there is real interaction between the structure of these theory groups and the kind of work they produce" (1984, 11).

I believe it is important to analyze Brym and Fox's text for several reasons. English Canadian sociology has not been overly reflexive in the past, in part because of the inductionist and positivistic biases of key practitioners. John Porter, perhaps English Canada's most widely known and read sociologist, expresses a viewpoint which seems prevalent. He writes, "the facts often speak for themselves, regardless of the framework within which they are presented" (Porter 1975, x).[1] In the 1970s and 1980s Canadian sociologists, armed with just such a philosophy, were feverishly involved in eliciting more "facts" about particular subject areas. The Brym with Fox book represents one of the few, and one of the more ambitious, attempts to analyze the sociological enterprise in Canada over the last thirty years. However, the book claims to be more comprehensive than it actually is. By topic, it covers only certain fields relating to economic development and under-development, politics and social movements, stratification and the feminist challenge to "malestream" sociology. This choice is justified by Brym as comparing "the main controversies that have animated sociology in English-Canada since the 1960s" (1989, 1). He claims such topics are among "the chief foci of English-Canadian sociologists today" (ibid., 2). He also suggests that he is being "governed" by an objective response to "the results of several reports that show where English-Canadian sociologists concentrate their research and teaching efforts" (ibid.).

This explanation seems unlikely as the fields chosen for discussion overlap with Brym's own areas of publication. A glance at his own works listed in the references (1989, 184-85) reveals that he has published in each of these fields except feminist sociology. Many sociologists in Canada will wonder if other fields were of less interest. The emergence of a radical-critical criminology will amaze anyone who remembers the empiricist-functionalist bias of the subdiscipline even into the 1970s. The emergence of a solid core of critical Canadian criminologists who have established a strong tradition of their own (signalled by the call at the 1989 Ontario Association of Sociology and Anthropology meeting by Carleton's Tullio Caputo to undertake a redefinition of such critical criminologists as no longer a beleaguered minority but as a new mainstream) seems as important as anything Brym chooses to discuss. This is not to say that the Brym-

Fox book is anything but excellent. It reads very lucidly, comments intelligently on a veritable mass of material relating to recent Canadian sociology (it cites no fewer than 148 journal articles by currently practising Canadian sociologists, not to mention books and research reports) and does so in a volume which is easily usable. It is sure to become, and deserves to be, a classic of its type.

However it is my contention—one taken from the sociology of knowledge and postmodernist debates—that there is no final "positivistic" presentation of reality, and that, in some way or another, all social science is about "representation" as it is constructed in the mind of the scientist-sociologist, as is the case with "facts" (see White 1978; Aronowitz 1988; Murphy 1988).

Regionalism and the Production of Canadian Sociology

One enduring contributor to polarization in Canada is regionalism. It is such a prominant feature of Canadian society that it seems odd to find a cognate Commonwealth country—New Zealand—depreciates the factor of regionalism on the grounds that "social conditions for the formation of distinctly separate regions do not exist" (Crothers 1984, 375).

In Canada the regional differences in population, language and ethnic origin, climate, size, political traditions and type of economic base are such that they have a major impact on Canadian identity. It is no accident that one complete chapter in Harry Hiller's *Canadian Society: A Macroanalysis* (1986) is devoted to regionalism and that it follows closely behind the issues of national dependency and inequality. Hiller makes the point that regionalism is "also a consequence of a *comparative-relationship* among regions . . . [and that] *power relationships* become obvious" (1986, 107).

Although Canadian sociologists have paid a great deal of attention to the issue of regionalism in Canadian society, this issue has not been noticed to any great degrees in relation to sociological production in Canada. In part this has to do with the underdeveloped state of the sociology of sociology in Canada. In part it may be due to an empiricist notion that publication decisions are simply reflex responses to the quality and quantity of what is submitted. Also the fact that the majority of sociologists are not indigenous to their region of employment must play a role.

In the United States this issue of regionalism, unequal power and publication rates are discussed by Straus and Radel (1969). Their interest in the topic was roused by a revision to the constitution of the American Sociological Association which had been stimulated in part "by the objection of sociologists in certain regions to what was believed to be a regional bias in the control of the association" (Straus and Radel 1969, 1). The authors were surprised that the issue was raised "without benefit of empirical data" and this they wished to provide. They found that there was some deviation from a regionally balanced ASA executive with such leaders coming disproportionately from the Pacific and Mountain and Northeast regions, with the Midwest and the South underrepresented (ibid., 2). The authors go beyond this finding to the issue of publication by region as they assume that "officeholding . . . is not expected to be strictly representative" and that "professional eminence" plays a role and "it is quite clear that centers of professional excellence are not equally distributed by region" (ibid.). They found that the Northeast was most productive followed "fairly closely" by the Pacific and Mountain regions and the Midwest, followed rather distantly by the South. On the basis of a citation count, the pattern was the same with the Northeast and the Pacific-Mountain states at the top, with the Midwest a close third, and the South far behind. The conclusions from this study were that, although election to higher ASA office was somewhat related to productivity, the Midwest had been overlooked, "severely underrepresented" as the authors put it (ibid., 4), in relation to the more important ASA offices, despite the high publication rates.

Ironically, this overlooking of the Midwest was to allow for some representation of Southerners at the highest levels (despite the average lower publication rate of the latter region). The article concludes by raising the question of why an equity principle of representation should have been achieved "at the expense of the Midwest rather than the other regions" but states that the answer is "unclear" (ibid., 4). It seems important to note that the Midwest was a *close* third in terms of publication rates and citations, in contrast to the more distant South.

In the current study of citations in Brym with Fox, the data is broken down into the following regions: the Atlantic provinces, Anglophone Québec, the Core Five universities in Ontario (Toronto, York, OISE's Department of Sociology in Education, McMaster, Carleton), the rest of Ontario, the Prairies, and British Columbia. In distinguishing the Core Five universities in Ontario from the rest of Ontario, I am influenced by Arthur K. Davis' article on hinterland-metropolis. He defines metropolises as "the centres of economic and political control located in the larger cities" and hinter-lands as "relatively underdeveloped colonial areas which export for the most part semi-processed extractive materials" (1971, 12). Davis is careful to identify "hierarchies of metropolis-hinterland relationships" and to view the metropolis-hinterland distinction "as a *series* of opposition" (ibid.).

Seen from this perspective, it makes sense to define Toronto and Ottawa as the core of economic and political power. From a professional point of view, these cities and Hamilton all have urban populations of over half a million, each of the departments in the Core Five has a doctoral program with many graduate students, and each university has or is very close to major libraries. The University of Ottawa has not been counted with the Core Five as its department is heavily francophone and, more importantly, it does not have a doctoral program.

Divided up in this fashion, we find 25 percent of English Canada's sociologists in the Core Five, the rest of Ontario accounts for about the same, the Prairies for a little less at 24.2 percent, the Atlantic region for 14.6 percent, and BC and Anglophone Québec for 5.8 and 5.1 percent respectively. The total number of sociologists in English Canada at universities seems to have remained constant since the mid 1970s to the present at just over 700. I depended in this analysis on the 1986 National Museum's Guide to Sociologists and Anthropologists in Canada (Herman 1986). I think this is justified on the grounds that the kernel of the Brym with Fox book originated in a 1986 monograph published by Brym alone in *Current Sociology* in 1986. Brym has updated and extended his text somewhat since then, and Fox's contribution was written after 1986. Where the National Museum overlooked a number of English Canadian sociologists at the university level and sociology departments, I have added them to the analysis (such as Athabaska University, Algoma and Nipissing University Colleges, University College of Cape Breton). Although I am aware that a number of sociologists have found employment at community colleges, it has not been necessary to consider them as Brym and Fox have been rather traditional in citing university-based sociologists operating in sociology departments.

I would like to begin by discussing Tables 1 and 2 which show the pattern of citation in Brym and Fox by individually named sociologist. Table 1 shows by sociologist the number of pages on which a sociologist is named; Table 2 shows the number of each sociologist's studies (individual articles, books, research reports, chapters) cited by Brym and Fox. The second table is somewhat complicated by the pattern of co- or multiple-authored studies. I have counted in all studies in which an individual is named as one of the authors.

Just over one hundred sociologists are cited at least once. The number of studies cited per person ranges from one to a high of sixteen, and the number of pages a person is cited on ranges from one to thirty-seven (Table 1). It may come as no surprise that from Table 1 we see that the Canadian sociologists cited on the greatest number of pages was John Porter, with S.D. Clark and Wallace Clement in a top group. However, the high rankings of some other individuals may be more controversial (such as the authors themselves) especially if anyone maintains an empiricist argument that such patterns of citation are a mirror of the pattern of production. In all about 14 to 15 percent of English Canadian sociologists are cited at least once. Of course many English Canadian sociologists

Table 1

Number of Pages Mentioning each Sociologist in *From Culture to Power*

37   John Porter
21   Michael Ornstein
18   S.D. Clark, B.J. Fox, W. Clement
17   R.J. Brym
12   W.K. Carroll
11   J. Fox, M. Boyd, J. Curtis
08   M. Cohen, C. Cuneo
07   P. Pineo, P. Connelly, R. Breton, J. Goyder
06   W. Kalbach, D. Magill, (including Wilcox-Magill), M. Luxton,R. Ogmundson,
     P. Ghorayshi, G. Laxer, G. Darroch, J. Reitz,M. Porter
05   M. Pinard, H. Hiller, J. Myles, A. Richmond, [J. Niosi]
04   H. Friedmann, A.A. Hunter, W. McVey, D. Olsen, H. Rich
03   K. Anderson, P. Armstrong, H. Armstrong, V. Burstyn, D. Dasko, M. Eichler,
     M. Gillespie, J.P. Grayson, Roberta Hamilton, B. Neis
02   R. Apostle, D. Clairmount, C.A. Dawson, C. Gannage, J. Gaskell, N. Guppy,
     Richard Hamilton, J. Harp, I.C. Jarvie, Wm. Johnston, R. Lambert, C.M.
     Lanphier, R. Lenton, P. Li, T. Makabe, J.G. Morgan, M. O'Brien, J. Sacouman,
     D.E. Smith, D. Stasiulis, P. Stevenson, K.W. Taylor. L. Tepperman, F.G.
     Vallee, B. Wellman, D.R. Whyte, S.D. Berkowitz, R. Morris
Source: Brym with Fox 1989.

Table 2

Number of Studies Authored or Co-authored as listed in the references
of *From Culture to Power* by Sociologist

16   M. Ornstein
15   R.J. Brym
09   R. Breton, J. Curtis
08   B.J. Fox, W.K. Carroll
07   R. Ogmundson, S.D. Clark
06   M. Boyd, G. Darroch, A. Richmond
05   P. Pineo, M. Pinard, J. Fox
04   W. Clement, C. Cuneo, J. Goyder, Marilyn Porter, J. Reitz, H. Hiller, J. Myles,
     B. Blishen, D.E. Smith
03   J. Porter, P. Connelly, G. Laxer, T. Makabe, Roberta Hamilton, Richard
     Hamilton, P. Armstrong, C.A. Dawson, P. Stevenson, D. Magill
Source: Brym with Fox 1989.

publish nothing which is directly relevant to the study of Canada, or publish nothing at all, so that the total number of persons cited as a proportion of the actual pool of English Canadian sociologists who have published items relevant to the study of Canadian society would be much higher.

Table 3

The Regional Distribution of the 10 and 29 Most-Cited English Canadian
Sociologists in *From Culture to Power* (based on page citations, Table 1)

Region	General Distribution (%)	10 most-cited (%)	29 most -cited (%)
Core Five	25.0	80	65.5
Prairies	24.2	0	10.3
Rest of Ontario	25.4	10	6.9
Atlantic	14.6	0	6.9
British Columbia	5.8	10	6.9
Anglophone Québec	5.1	0	3.4

Percentages have been rounded. Source: Brym with Fox 1989; Herman 1986.

Table 3 looks at the top ten and the top twenty-nine most cited
sociologists in Brym and Fox as measured by the number of pages an
author is cited on. Eighty percent of the top ten most cited sociologists and
almost two-thirds (65.5 percent) of the top twenty-nine come from the
Core Five universities. This is compared to their actual share of all sociologists in English Canada—25 percent. By this measure, the Prairies, the rest
of Ontario and the Atlantic provinces are all considerably under-cited
compared to their general distribution. The top ten most cited sociologists
are cited on at least ten pages of text, the top twenty-nine on at least five
pages of text.

Table 4

Percentage of Total Sociologists in each Region Cited
in *From Culture to Power* (cited at least once)

Region	% Cited in Brym and Fox
Core Five	.27
Atlantic	.18
Anglophone Quebec	.17
British Columbia	.10
Rest of Ontario	.08
Prairies	.06
Canada	.15

Source: Brym with Fox 1989; Herman 1986.

Table 4 shows regional citation in Brym and Fox in terms of the
percentage of faculty in each region who are cited at all (that is on at least
one page) in *From Culture to Power*. Thus 27 percent of the Core Five
sociology faculty are cited, 18 percent of the Atlantic sociologists, 17
percent of those from Anglophone Québec, 10 percent of those from

Table 5

Journals Cited in *From Culture to Power* by Number of Articles
and by Geographical Location

Canada	Number of Articles Cited
Canadian Review of Sociology and Anthropology	65
Canadian Journal of Sociology	26
Studies in Political Economy	09
Canadian Ethnic Studies	03
Journal of Canadian Studies	02
Atlantis	02
Society-société	02
CHA Historical Papers	02
Canadian Historical Review	01
Labour	01
Queen's Quarterly	01
Sociologie et sociétés	01
Newfoundland Studies	01
Alternate Routes	01
Canada	**117**

Foreign	
American Journal of Sociology	04
Social Forces	03
American Sociological Review	02
Sociological Focus	02
The American Sociologist	02
Sociology Inquiry	02
Comparative Social Research	02
British Journal of Sociology	01
Signs	01
Administrative Sciences Quarterly	01
Sociological Analysis	01
Ethnicity	01
Current Sociology	01
The Insurgent Sociologist	01
Comparativ Studies in Society and History	01
International Migration Review	01
Journal for the History of the Behavioral Sciences	01
Social Science Information	01
Studies in Comparative International Development	01
Research in Social Structure and Mobility	01
Population Studies	01
Foreign	**31**

Source: Brym with Fox 1989.

British Columbia, 8 percent in the rest of Ontario and only 6 percent of sociologists from the Prairie provinces are cited. The average for all sociologists in English Canada is 15 percent. Thus the Core Five sociologists are more than 400 percent more likely to be cited at least once than Prairie sociologists and about 300 percent more than their colleagues in the rest of Ontario. What is valid is to compare each regional percentage with the Canadian average of 15. Basically all sociologists north and west of Toronto are under-cited including, perhaps surprisingly, those in British Columbia and outside of the metropolitan core in Ontario. On the other hand, Anglophone Québec and the Atlantic provinces are slightly "over-cited" in terms of their general distribution.

Empiricists may retort that such a pattern of citation is simply a mirror reflection of relevant publications. One way to estimate this is by looking at regional rates of publication in the *Canadian Review of Sociology and Anthropology* and *The Canadian Journal of Sociology* (referred to as the *CRSA* and the *CJS* henceforth).

Table 6

Canadian Journal of Sociology 1975-1988 and Canadian Review of Sociology and Anthropology 1975-1984 by Author'sRegion

Region	General Distribution (%)	CJS(%)	CRSA(%)
Core Five	25.0	31.8	35.9
Prairies	24.2	28.0	22.7
Rest of Ontario	25.4	18.4	20.5
Atlantic	14.6	10.7	10.0
British Columbia	5.8	8.0	7.3
Anglo Quebec	5.1	3.3	3.6

The percentages have been rounded. Sources: Herman 1986; Indexes 1986 and 1989 for The Canadian Review of Sociology and Anthropology and The Canadian Journal of Sociology.

The total number of articles cited from each journal is shown in Table 5. Thus the majority of articles cited in Brym and Fox authored by Canadian sociologists were published in *CRSA* and *CJS*. It might be argued that Canadian sociologists were publishing more prestigiously elsewhere but, as the table shows, only relatively few articles cited by Brym and Fox appeared in the *American Journal of Sociology* or the *American Sociological Review*. As Table 5 demonstrates, whereas one hundred articles cited in Brym and Fox came from the top three most cited Canadian journals, only nine were cited from the American trio of *ASR, AJS, Social Forces* and *ASR*.

In Table 6 articles cited from the two core Canadian journals are divided according to the region of the author. In this table it *is* valid to compare the left and right columns and make a comparison. It might be argued that Core Five publication rates are three to four hundred percent higher in the two major English Canadian journals on the basis of their level of citation. Table 6 shows that this is not the case, although it is true that there is some overrepresentation of Core Five authors. This is most marked for the *CRSA*. However, it is clear from these data that although Prairie and the rest of Ontario authors are *somewhat* underrepresented in the *CRSA*, this scarcely amounts to a discrepancy of three or four hundred percent. In the case of the *CJS*, both the Core and Prairie authors are somewhat overrepresented. The drastic underrepresentation of Prairie authors noted in Brym and Fox may in part be due to their relative neglect of the *CJS* compared to the *CRSA*. Brym alone authored or co-authored three papers in the *CJS*, thus only 21 *CJS* papers by other authors were cited. However, to get back to the main point, the Prairies and the rest of Ontario were only slightly below the general distribution but were drastically under-cited in Brym and Fox. On the other hand, Atlantic sociologists were somewhat underrepresented in both the *CRSA* and the *CJS* but were slightly over-cited in Brym and Fox.

Personal Networks and Theory Groups
Turning aside from regional considerations, let us review one article by Diana Crane which goes beyond empiricist-positivist assumptions about the construction of knowledge: "The Gatekeepers of Science: Some Factors Affecting the Selection of Articles for Scientific Journals" (1967, 194-201). This article looks at the practices of journal editors in the social sciences (sociology, economics) and in the case of the *American Sociological Review* did so before and after anonymous refereeing was introduced in 1955. She finds that "the evaluation of scientific articles is affected to some degree by non-scientific factors" (ibid., 200). She suggests two such factors which might apply: "editorial readers respond to certain aspects of methodology, theoretical expression and mode of expression in the writings of those who have received similar training"; and "doctoral training and academic affiliations influence personal ties between scientists which in turn influence their evaluation of scientific work . . . " (ibid.).

Another extra-scientific factor which Crane investigates is the "unearned increment" which is accorded to minimally productive colleagues at major universities: "Evidently, productivity did not make the scientist as visible to . . . colleagues . . . as did a position at a major university" (1965, 710). Her study reveals that high producers at minor universities received only slightly more recognition than low producers at major universities and far less than high producers at major universities (ibid., Table 10). Crane herself talks about a possible "halo" effect that a major university confers on work even if on the basis of the substance it may be undeserved. Thus, to use her term, "non-scientific factors" do come into play in the construction of what is accepted as legitimate knowledge and in the construction of scientific reputations.

The citation pattern of Brym and Fox is consistent with Crane's finding. The Core Five universities are located in the major metropolitan centres of economic and political power, all have complete graduate programs up to the doctoral level. The two authors themselves are from the Core Five universities and they, along with the husband of one (John Fox), are represented among the top ten most cited authors by number of pages (Table 1). Michael Ornstein, who emerges as one of the top two most cited sociologists from Tables 1 and 2, was the supervisor of the seventh most cited (for William Carroll's PhD dissertation) and was a former collaborator with John Fox. Robert Brym acted as an examiner of Gordon Laxer's dissertation, one of the ninth most cited.

Rather than referring to personal networks influenced by friendship and kinship, let us look at the pattern of citation as evinced among University of Toronto and University of Alberta doctoral graduates. Both of these universities have had large doctoral programs since the mid 1960s. Robert Brym received his doctoral degree from the University of Toronto in 1976, spent two years at the Memorial University in Newfoundland, and then became a faculty member at Toronto in 1978. Fox received her PhD from Alberta in 1980, but spent a minimal amount of time there. She taught at several universities in several regions until her appointment with the University of Toronto in 1985. While Brym is clearly tied to the Toronto connection, this is less clear with Fox.

Between 1967 and 1984, 81 PhDs were awarded by Alberta compared to 130 by Toronto. Between 1973 and 1984, the numbers were 69 and 112 respectively. Table 7 shows that Brym and Fox were twice as likely to cite PhD graduates from Toronto as from Alberta, thus 10 percent of Toronto's total number of doctoral graduates between 1967 and 1984 are cited at least once in Brym and Fox, as opposed to just about 5 percent of Alberta graduates. In the period from 1973 to 1984 when Brym would have known many of the Toronto graduate students personally, the percentage goes up to almost 12 percent compared to just under 6 percent for those with Alberta PhDs.

Even when Alberta doctoral graduates wrote on topics very relevant to *From Culture to Power* such as Heather-Jo Hammer's dissertation "Mature Dependency: The Effects of American Direct Investment on Canadian

Economic Growth" (1983-84), they were likely to be ignored by Brym and Fox in spite, in the case of Hammer, of being published in prestigious journals (Hammer and Gartrell 1986). One of the four Alberta graduates cited in Brym and Fox (not counting Fox) was A.R. Gillis, a colleague of the authors at the University of Toronto and thus within their orbit of proximity and connections.

Table 7

Pattern of Citation in *From Culture to Power* by Location of Doctoral Degree, Universities of Alberta and Toronto

University	Dates	PhD Graduates	Number Cited	As a %
Alberta	1973-1984	69	4	5.7
Toronto		112	13	11.6
Alberta	1967-1984	81	4	4.9
Toronto		130	13	10.0

Sources: Helmes-Hayes 1988; Department of Sociology, University of Alberta 1984.

Once more the empiricist may suggest that the pattern of citations is simply a mirror reflection of the "state of the art." One way to examine this issue, besides considering publication in the two major English Canadian sociology journals, would be to consider citations. The best and most available measure is the *Social Science Citation Index.* There are some criticisms of this tool in the literature particularly regarding its representation of Canadian scholarship (Assheton-Smith 1979, 52). However, it is commonly used as an indicator of esteem, prestige, and even of that elusive concept in the social sciences, quality.

Jonathan and Stephen Cole, two well known contributors to the sociology of science and knowledge, write, "The data available indicate that straight citation counts are highly correlated with virtually every refined measure of quality . . . the value of using them as rough indicators of the quality of a scientist's work should not be overlooked" (1971, 28).

Using *SSCI* cites, is, for the Coles, a means to measure quality which relies on Kuhn's recognition that science is a social construction. In other words, they proceed from the view that it is impossible to ascertain "absolute truth"; instead, truth in scientific work is that which is considered useful by scientific colleagues (Cole and Cole 1973, 24).

They also go on to argue against the view that critical citations indicate a lack of quality in authors so criticized. For the Coles, "all publicity is good publicity" in the sense that criticized work is work that has still been found useful in the advancement of science (ibid., 25). They suggest that it is "unlikely . . . that work which is valueless will be deemed significant enough to merit extensive criticism. If a paper presents an error which is important enough to elicit frequent criticism, the paper, though erroneous, is probably a significant contribution. The significance of a paper is not necessarily determined by its correctness" (ibid.). This is a rather important point to consider given the fact that most of the citations in Brym with Fox of Porter, Clement and the Carleton School are critical in nature despite their high placing in Tables 1 and 2. It is perhaps difficult to agree with the Coles that the number of citations of an author is itself a sufficient indicator of objective quality since it seems clear that the number of citations in any field depends partly on the number of researchers in the field and partly on whether a particular text partakes in the popular assumptions of any given age. Thus, other things being equal, articles dealing with North American and British studies in those parts of the world will be more frequently cited than in those dealing with Danish or Costa Rican studies. Measures of citations do indicate the extent to which a person's work is known and found useful in a particular scholarly community.

The Coles present some evidence to counter such criticisms of citation measures. They found that "at least in physics" there was "no relationship between the size of a specialty and the number of citations to the work of men in that specialty" (1973, 29). According to the Coles, in 1966 there were 4,593 solid-state physicists and only 1,833 elementary particle physicists. Yet the latter group actually had a few more citations, on the average, than the larger group. However the Coles did recognize the issue of size as possibly relevant (ibid., 28). It may be that research in the humanities and social sciences differs since it does do not necessarily use the building block method of natural science.

There are a number of strange anomalies in the pattern of citation in *From Culture to Power*. Perhaps the strangest is the complete failure to cite the work of Patricia Marchak, a former president of the Canadian Sociology and Anthropology Association. Between 1981 and 1989, she garnered eighty-eight citations in the *SSCI* which puts her in a category above Brym himself (especially when it is remembered that about half of Brym's seventy-one *SSCI* citations are to topics *not* relevant to Canadian macrosociology). This absence is also surprising since Marchak has published on most of the topics relevant to *From Culture to Power*. Furthermore, it should be pointed out that Marchak was a presenter at the conference on "The Structure of the Canadian Capitalist Class," held at the University of Toronto in November 1983. Brym was a member of the organizing group behind this conference, and was the editor of the two volumes which came from it. Marchak's article from the conference was published in the second of the two volumes (Marchak 1986).

The omission of certain authors by Brym and Fox despite their prominence in the *SSCI* at times is due to the selectivity of topics discussed earlier. Thus Reginald Bibby, Canada's most cited sociologist of religion with seventy *SSCI* cites and Kenneth Westhues with forty-three, remain uncited although both authors have published material relevant to Canadian macrosociology. Other western authors not cited in Brym and Fox despite many *SSCI* citations or important publications include Alan B. Anderson (forty), John Conway (seventeen), Arthur K. Davis (twenty-seven), James Frideres (fifty-five), Marlene M. Mackie (sixty-one), and Emily Nett (sixteen). In another case, a distinguished author on ethnic studies, Leo Driedger with seventy-four *SSCI* citations, is quoted on only one page of Brym and Fox, while J. Reitz, a Toronto colleague of Brym's interested in ethnic studies with forty-eight *SSCI* cites, is mentioned on six pages.

Another point worth discussing is the disregard of Prairie authors even when they publish articles relevant to the topics chosen by Brym and Fox, and even when such articles are in sources close to hand. Thus Harry H. Hiller's "Internal Party Resolution and Third Party Emergence" in the *Canadian Journal of Sociology* (1977) is not cited, nor is James McCrorie's article "Change and Paradox in Agrarian Social Movements" or Arthur K. Davis's chapter "Canadian Society and History as Hinterland Versus Metropolis," both published in Richard Ossenberg's book, *Canadian Society* (1971). The article by Davis has been reprinted several times and as recently as 1990 in a reader (Curtis and Tepperman); between 1976 and 1985 it was cited twenty-four times in the *SSCI*. John Conway's articles on populism, published in the *Journal of Canadian Studies* (1979) and the *Canadian Journal of Political Science* (1978), are also not cited; the same is the case for his book on *The West* (1983b).

Brym is not ignorant of these articles as most of them are cited, but not quoted, in his article on "Social Movements and Third Parties" in *Models and Myths in Canadian Society* (1984). Conway's *The West* is an entry in an annotated bibliography by Brym (1986b, 208). In some cases, the failure to cite in *From Culture to Power* may be due to theoretical or methodological considerations. Thus a paragraph on page twenty-three could well be said to summarize A.K. Davis's views without mentioning his name.

The method followed in this chapter may be applied generally to other works in sociology. If the assumptions of the sociology of knowledge are correct—that knowledge is a social enterprise in which social factors play a role in determining what constitutes knowledge, then similar findings should be arrived at when works other than *From Culture to Power* are considered, such as, for example, the second edition of Robert Stebbins' volume *Sociology: The Study of Society* (1990). Stebbins teaches at the University of Calgary and is a former president of the Canadian Sociology and Anthropology Association. He is originally from the United States and has a PhD from Minnesota, but has worked in Canada since 1965, except for three years in Texas. He was at the Memorial University of Newfoundland from 1965 to 1973, before he moved to his current location in 1976 (Jaques Cattell Press 1978, 1144).

Table 8 shows the pattern of citation for eight English Canadian sociologists who were cited on three or more pages. Table 9 shows the regional breakdown for those cited on five pages or more, considering the nine and then twenty-five most cited authors. The lists of Canadian sociologists were taken from the American Sociological Association's 1989

Table 8

Number of Pages Mentioning each Sociologist in R. Stebbins' *Sociology*.

20	R. Stebbins
9	J. Porter
6	E. Lupri, J. Frideres, A. Hunter, W.B.W. Martin
5	R. Bibby, M. Mackie, R. Prus
4	P. Pineo, H. Hiller, W. Clement, R.J. Brym
3	J. Hagan, J.D. House, M. Boyd, M. Eichler, J.P. Grayson, N. Guppy, H. McRoberts, P. Marchak, A.B. Anderson, G.S. Lowe, F. Elkin, A.J. Macdonell

Source: Stebbins 1990.

Table 9

Regional Distribution of the 9 and 25 Most-Cited English Canadian Sociologists in R. Stebbins' *Sociology*.

Region	General Distribution (%)	Most-Cited 9 (%)	Most-Cited 25 (%)
Core Five	24.8	22.2	44
Prairies	23.3	55.6	32
Rest of Ontario	25.5	11.1	4
Atlantic	14.6	11.1	12
British Columbia	6.0	0	8
Anglophone Québec	5.8	0	0

Sources: Stebbins 1990; ASA Guide to Graduate Departments 1989; Commonwealth Universities Yearbook 1988.

Guide to Graduate Departments, supplemented by the *Commonwealth Universities Yearbook 1988* and a few individual university calendars when necessary.

According to Table 9, the Prairies, far from being grossly under-cited, are considerably over-cited compared to the general distribution in Canada. The Core is actually a little under-cited, at least in terms of the statistical figure for the nine most-cited They again are over-cited in the next column. The rest of Ontario, the Atlantic region, BC, and Anglophone Québec are all under-cited to varying degrees. However, it should be noted that the Atlantic region is only marginally under-cited; it may be relevant to remember that Stebbins spent a number of years there in the early 1970s. The three Atlantic sociologists cited among the top twenty-five are all veterans in the area. A.J. Macdonell was hired by the University of New Brunswick in 1971, and House and Martin were both listed in the 1978 edition of the National Museum's *Guide to Departments* (Herman and Carstens 1979). (It should be noted for the benefit of those who wish to replicate these tables that S.D. Clark is listed in the index as cited on three pages but this is incorrect as one of the citations is a work by his son, Samuel D. Clark, a member of the department of sociology at Western.) The point of the above analysis is to show that the effects of region and personal network are not unusual, but are frequent and common. No doubt collectively-authored readers for introductory sociology in Canada are favoured, in part, to overcome such effects.

Conclusion

In examining these examples of sociological writing, it is clear that geographical location, personal networks including graduate school, methodological and theoretical biases, and the reputation of authors all intersect in dictating which authors are cited and which are not. Sociologists who are physically close to Brym and Fox, who are at departments distinguished by their relative largeness and by advanced graduate programs, who write on topics of interest to the authors in approved styles, are likely to be cited. "Out of sight, out of mind" is a maxim not entirely out of place in the context of *From Culture to Power*. Yet we notice that Atlantic authors are cited somewhat more than what their number (Table 4) would warrant and three hundred percent as much as Prairie authors.

It is my contention that this pattern of citations hardly represents a mirror image of sociological production given the emphasis on research at several large Prairie universities such as Calgary, Alberta, Manitoba and, increasingly, Saskatchewan. Rather, it has a lot to do with Brym's own background. He was brought up in New Brunswick, received his BA and MA from Dalhousie, was as a faculty member at Memorial for two years,

and played a prominent role in giving rise to a political economy orientation in Atlantic research (Brym and Sacouman, 1979).

In Chapter One I discuss how the sociology of knowledge now acknowledges the social nature of the production of knowledge and rejects
extreme empiricist and positivist views. It is likely that much if not all of
the empirics of this chapter will be a surprise to authors who may suppose
that factors of objective merit or intrinsic interest alone influence their
citation decisions. There is no reason to suppose that sociological authors
themselves are clear in their own minds about the rationale of citation
choices. But if the sociology of knowledge's analysis of sociology itself is
valid (as it claims it is), we should be wary of accepting any sociological
interpretation as the final word regarding our social world. All writing is
hermeneutic, all writing is selective, all writing proceeds through conceptual filters of one sort or another. One hardly expects the citation patterns
or interpretation or cognitive evaluations of a Dorothy E. Smith to be those
of a Talcott Parsons, but perhaps it will still surprise us that these aspects
in an account produced by two centrally located core sociologists with
extensive Atlantic experience differ from the more western citations of a
Harry Hiller, a John Conway, a Patricia Marchak or a James McCrorie.

As far as the specific implications for readers of the Brym and Fox text
is concerned, my conclusion is not to suggest that the book should be
avoided (as all books are written from specific social locations), rather the
regional, personal and professional choices of the authors should be kept
clearly in mind when assessing and evaluating this particular rendering of
Canadian sociology. Recognizing the validity of such an exercise shows, I
believe, the relevance of the sociology of knowledge to understanding
sociology itself.

Note

[1] For a more explicit and philosophical treatment of the nature of science from an
empiricist-positivistic standpoint see Nettler (1970), especially on "Scientific Explanation," pp.85-111.

Chapter Six

E.F. Wilson and the Social Construction of Text

Previous chapters have indicated how social factors influenced a number of prominent Canadian sociologists—S.D. Clark, John Porter, Robert Brym, Bonnie Fox. It is not my suggestion that such social influences can be avoided. I agree with Ludwik Fleck, as previously cited, that "without social conditioning no cognition is even possible" (1979, 43).

In order to illustrate this principle more clearly, I have decided to show the social influences on my own socio-historical work dealing with the missionary E.F. Wilson. In doing so, I also discuss the writings by Peter Moore and Paulette Jiles about E.F. Wilson as the only other texts on Wilson known to me at the time of writing.

In providing this introduction to my own writing on Wilson, I add one warning: when summarized in this fashion, the analysis may infer that I had a road-map to follow in approaching Wilson's life before I even began to write. This is far from the truth. Writing the following piece on my own influences and motivations only came after the finished product (especially the book of 1988). This later reflection on my own socio-historical production has helped to illumine the entire process even to me, the author. In other words, the entire process of motivation and influence is largely subconscious and hidden at the time of creation, and I doubt that it can be otherwise except in the most propagandistic of work.

Historical Discourse and Epistemology

During most of the nineteenth and twentieth centuries historians adopted much of the positivist conception of science in their practice. History, in this view, was an inductive pursuit which depended on the unearthing of masses of facts. The historical researcher could and should be separated in interest from the subject at hand. Subjects such as the philosophy of history were roundly condemned by the new "scientific" historians because it was felt that philosophers of history contaminated their analysis with preconceptions.

Such a view was voiced by Henri Houssaye who spoke at the First International Congress of Historians in 1900. He wanted "nothing more to do with the approximation of hypotheses, useless systems, theories as brilliant as they are deceptive, superfluous moralities. Facts, facts, facts— which carry within themselves their lesson and their philosophy" (Novick 1988, 38). Albert Bushnell Hart, in a presidential address to the American Historical Association in 1910, called for "a genuinely scientific school of history" which would imitate Charles Darwin in spending twenty years accumulating data before venturing a generalization. This scientific method would be "inductive" and would proceed by relentless observation "of the grain in its narrow spout" (ibid.). Edward Cheyney, writing at the turn of the century, stated that the "simple but arduous task of the historian was to collect facts, view them objectively, and arrange them as the facts them- selves demanded" (ibid., 38-39). He objected to "beginning the examina- tion of historical facts . . . with any theory of interpretation" (ibid.) In another address in 1907, Cheyney said that the historian's "design already exists, the events have actually occurred, the past has really been—his task is to approach as near to the design as he possibly can" (ibid., 56).

One result of the scientific view of history was the sanctification of the idea that the observer could and should be disconnected emotionally from her or his subject. This denigrated of philosophies of history as the "scien- tific" historians held that such attempts represented "the effort to write history on the basis of philosophical preconceptions which required the bending of the evidence of the scheme arrived at by a prioristic reasoning" (White 1973, 141). Another consequence was vigorous denial of any sug- gestion that historians use "facts" in the framework of literacy devices and conventions. This distinction between history and fiction was "the most sacred boundary of all" (Novick 1988, 600). The "scientific" historian felt if one went to the archives "without any preconception whatsoever" that historical explanation would "emerge naturally from the documents them- selves" (White 1973, 141).

According to historian Peter Novick, the assumptions of "scientific" history were significantly challenged in the 1920s and 1930s by several prominent historians such as Carl Becker and Charles Beard, and by a social attitude which undergirded such developments. The gist of their criticism was that "the selection and organization of facts was an act of purposeful thought by the historian, controlled, in Beard's words, by a frame of reference composed of 'things deemed necessary, things deemed possible, and things deemed desirable' " (Novick 1988, 255). Reliance upon "fact" was not the definitive route since "deciding what was a fact . . . depended upon values" (ibid., 254). Since values vary by culture and by period, it would follow that historical accounts will differ for each genera- tion or subculture. This implication is captured in the title of Becker's 1931 presidential address to the American Historical Association: "Everyman

His Own Historian."

The presidential discourses of Becker (1931) and Beard (1933) certainly cannot be said to have been ignored. According to Novick, "no presidential addresses to the American Historical Association ever occasioned as much discussion" as these (Novick 1988, 258). Yet the "scientific" conception of history survived. Novick suggests that the anti-totalitarian struggle against Nazism and Stalinist communism and the recommencement of war were prominent reasons. As he puts it, "a period of negativity and doubt followed the First World War, and the Second World War "saw American culture turn toward affirmation and the search for certainty" (ibid., 280).

In the 1960s and 1970s, however, people in the West were ripe for the rebirth of a post-empiricist or post-positivistic epistemology. These times were characterized by scepticism, disillusionment and cynicism. Claims of some sort of complete, final or objectivistic truth seemed out of joint; debunking and unmasking pretensions seemed more in line with the predominating mood. The work of science historian Thomas Kuhn, *The Structure of Scientific Revolutions* (1962), had an enormous impact. In it he attacks the notion that scientists are swayed primarily by fact and argues instead that they are influenced primarily by pre-established and uncritically accepted models or paradigms. In France in the 1960s and 1970s postmodernism and poststructuralism also began to have an impact, initially in the fields of literature and philosophy. However, in 1973 Hayden White's imposing volume, *Metahistory: The Historical Imagination in Nineteenth Century Europe* appeared, showing the influence of postmodernism and attacking the previously sacrosanct boundary drawn between history and literature.

Certainly for postmodernists the worship of "fact" as the bedrock of scientific history or social science has been dethroned and deconstructed. According to Hayden White, "We may seek to give our lives a meaning of some specific kind by telling now one and now another kind of story about them. But this is a work of deconstruction rather than of discovery . . . . Neither the reality nor the meaning of history is 'out there' in the form of a story awaiting only a historian to discern its outline and identify the plot that comprises its meaning" (cited in Novick 1988, 600). The historian presses "facts" into service in order to embellish a narrative structure; she or he does not stumble upon "facts" naively. Indeed, White suggests "there are no grounds to be found in the record itself for preferring one way of construing its meaning rather than another" (ibid., 601).

Drawing upon Canadian literary scholar Northrop Frye, White suggests that narratives identify "the *kind of story* that has been told" (White 1973, 7) through shaping the material by means of Tragedy, Romance,

Comedy and Satire. Romance is defined as "a drama of self-identification symbolized by the hero's transcendence of the world of experience, his victory over it, and his final liberation from it . . . . It is a drama of the triumph of good over evil, of virtue over vice, of light over darkness . . ." (ibid., 8-9). Satire is seen as the precise opposite of the Romantic mode: it recognizes that "man is ultimately a captive of the world rather than its master" (ibid., 9). In Comedy there is some hope for "the temporary triumph of man over his world" by occasional reconciliations symbolized by festive occasions. In Tragedy there are "no festive occasions" but intimations of "the fall of the protagonist and the shaking of the world he inhabits" (ibid.). This typology is referred to by White as "modes of emplotment."

White also suggests that historians will choose a mode of argument from among the formist, mechanistic, organicist and contextualist. These categories relate to the degree to which events are represented as particular and unique as opposed to the degree to which they are seen as part of greater processes. A final consideration which will be broached by each narrative (adapted from Karl Mannheim) is its mode of ideological impli-cation—anarchist, radical, conservative or liberal. Conservatives are "of course, the most suspicious of programmatic transformation of the social status quo" (ibid., 24). Radicals and anarchists both believe in the neces-sity for structural transformations, "the former in the interest of reconsti-tuting society on a new basis, the latter in the interest of abolishing society and substituting for it a 'community' of individuals held together by a shared sense of their common 'humanity' " (ibid., 24). Liberals seek change but view it as a result of adjustments or "fine tunings." Perhaps it should be added that these terms are meant to serve as "designators of general ideological preference rather than as emblems of specific political parties" (ibid.).

The Career of E.F. Wilson
In what follows I discuss three texts which deal with the nineteenth century Anglo-Canadian missionary and educator, E. F. Wilson. Wilson, born in 1844, came to Canada from England in 1865 hoping to be a farmer. He came from a distinguished Evangelical Anglican family which was dotted with clergy, pious business people, and even a missionary bishop (Wilson's grandfather had been Bishop of Calcutta from 1832 to 1858). Shortly after meeting the First Nations people of southern Ontario, Wilson became convinced that God wished he would undertake a mission to them. He abandoned farming, studied at Huron College in London, Ontario, and after some time back in England for ordination and marriage, set out again for southern Ontario. He returned as a missionary for the Church Mission-

ary Society, an evangelical missionary agency of the Church of England.

Wilson's mission to the Ojibway of southern Ontario was a troubled one, partly because of the differing views of the Church Missionary Society leader Henry Venn and the local bishop, Benjamin Cronyn. After several years of disappointments, but also of concrete effort, Wilson moved further north to Sault Ste. Marie and struck upon the idea of establishing a residential school for Native children. For many years there were actually two schools, one for boys and one for girls. Later he also established one other school at Elkhorn, Manitoba, and he had plans for still others.

In 1885, the Riel Rebellion spawned great interest in Wilson regarding the history and ethnology of the various First Nations peoples. He began to read, consult and correspond with leading anthropologists of the day; he also began to travel extensively to visit the various nations—the Cherokee in Oklahoma, the Pueblo and Zuni of the American southwest, the Blackfoot and Cree of the Prairies, and so on. Wilson became convinced that the program of cultural replacement and assimilation as practiced at schools and as encouraged by the Canadian government was not effective. He came to the view that political autonomy, self-government, and cultural synthesis might be a better strategy for Native advancement. His observation of the Cherokee, who followed such a policy and retained a *de facto* autonomous government until 1907, reinforced this view.

Despite such changes in his outlook, Wilson continued to support the building of schools which, with the increasing intrusion of the Federal government into the curriculum of the schools, were becoming even more thorough in promoting cultural replacement. Wilson was a man of action, rather than a systematic thinker, who wanted something done about the plight of Native peoples. By 1892 he had become discouraged in his work on both fronts. He ran into disputes about the running and control of the schools, and his plans to further Native self-government and cultural synthesis fell apart when a Native peoples' conference he promoted failed to be held. Faced with such disillusionment, combined with the ill health of his wife and the claims of his large family, he "retired" to become a very active pastor to Anglicans living on Salt Spring Island, BC, and a farmer. He died in 1915.

A Text From the 1950s

The work I wish to discuss to commence this consideration of the social construction of text was written by Peter B. Moore. It was completed in 1959 as part of his Bachelor of Theology at Huron College, an Anglican affiliate of the University of Western Ontario, London, Ontario. Moore's supervisor was J.H. Henderson, a prominent Canadian church historian. Peter B. Moore was a young man in his early twenties at this time studying for the Anglican ministry. He remains active in this profession in southern Ontario to this day. My argument is that Moore's text is a product of the times; the aspects of Wilson's life Moore chose to document were those which were esteemed in the 1950s by the author.

The dominant role of Moore's text is introduced in the unpaginated preface. The tone here is filiopietistic. That is to say, the writer admires the labours of Wilson and sees him as a type of role model worthy of emulation. He is identified as "a missionary priest" who exhibited "fervent devotion to his task" and who "despite his many set-backs persevered to the end . . ." (Moore 1959) His commitment represents for the writer "a source of inspiration" and the continuing existence of the Shingwauk residential school in 1959 "stands today as a living witness to his dedicated ministry." The "kind of story" being told, then, is one of Romance; despite many set-backs, the hero, because of the strength and purity of his character, is able to rise above them. This is a story of the "triumph of good over evil, of virtue over vice" and of the hero's "transcendence of the world."

A good example of this form of representation is Moore's discussion of the burning of the first Shingwauk School in 1873 only a week after it was completed. This disaster threatened Wilson's entire young mission, especially since he had decided to wait until its completion before taking out insurance. As Moore writes, "Less than a week after Wilson's dream had been partially realized, it was almost completely shattered" (1959,19). This event was followed shortly after by the death of one of his young daughters. Moore goes into considerable detail about Wilson's decision to begin again and his success in fundraising. The "moral" of the story is that Wilson was "supported by a wonderful spirit which carried him through many a difficulty which would have easily defeated many a man of less determination . . ." (ibid., 23). This point is sustained throughout the volume. Aside from the personal grit and determination of the hero endeavouring to overcome obstacles, Wilson's main motivation is held to be his steadfast devotion to divine service: "It was Edward Wilson's prime purpose in life to do everything he could, with the help of God, to extend the Kingdom of God among the Indians of Northern and Western Canada" (Moore 1959, 35).

The conclusion of Moore's thesis re-emphasizes the portrait of E.F. Wilson as a Romantic Hero exemplifying the triumph of good over evil and virtue over vice. His motivation is imputed to be his concern that a Native person should be able to "take his place in society" and be "received into the hearts of the Canadian people" (ibid., 59). Moore states that Wilson's name will "go down as one who conscientiously spent his days" so that Native people might "have a more abundant life" (ibid.). Wilson's career was difficult, but he was "continually upheld by an inner conviction" of God's providential concern (ibid.).

The story of Wilson's interest after 1885 in such ideas as Native self-government and retaining some elements of Native cultures (cultural synthesis if not cultural continuity) is not a subject of major interest to Moore. What is of major interest is the controversy over control and financing of the schools. In 1959, when Moore's text was completed, ideas about Native self-government and cultural synthesis were rarely expressed or contemplated. The assumption of assimilation and cultural replacement was still widely accepted in the dominant society. Thus Moore's representation of Wilson as an inspiring missionary and clerical figure was one in tune with the times. His later ideas, which very much went against the grain of conventional thinking, were left out of the picture.

I am inclined to suggest that the period between 1963 and 1980 represented a type of "quiet revolution" not just in Québec but in all of Canada. During this time Canada flew a new flag, moved away from Anglo-conformity to multiculturalism and bilingualism, and saw the first revival of organized challenges to patriarchy and the establishment of a major Royal Commission dealing with discrimination against women. Other important changes included a marked turning away from Christian bodies (signified by the title of Pierre Berton's *The Comfortable Pew* (1965) and their transformation from within, and a new militance among First Nations people in response to the termination policies of the White Paper of 1968-69. In a few short years the world and image mirrored in Peter B. Moore's text died away. The emphasis on moral rightness and transcendence over adversity in that text was far removed from the spirit of the late 1960s and 1970s, a new epoch which tended to debunk earlier values, institutions and motivations. It was no longer a period for a representation of E.F. Wilson as an exemplary clerical hero since unease in both the pulpit and pew and a new skepticism about the churches' missions replaced earlier concerns. Peter Novick writes of the new ethos: "the political culture lurched sharply left, then right: consensus was replaced first by polarization, then by fragmentation; affirmation by negativity, confusion, apathy, and uncertainty. . . " (1988, 415). The next text dealing with E.F. Wilson is that of Paulette Jiles, published in 1976.

A Text From the 1970s
Paulette Jiles is a poet, later a Governor-General's Award winner, who in the mid 1970s went to northwestern Ontario to work "with CBC's Department of Community Radio" (Jiles 1976, 15). She decided that as a matter of "common courtesy" and out of politeness she should try to learn the language of the people. To do so, she picks up Wilson's *Manual of the Ojebway Language*. She points out that "This is the only Ojibway grammar

available" (ibid.). It is ironic that, published as it was in 1874 as a primer for missionaries, it was reprinted as recently as 1975 by the Department of Indian Affairs and Northern Development. Perhaps the irony is not the satire into which Paulette Jiles dips her pen, but that by 1975 Ojibway scholarship had not become more extensive.

Jiles knows nothing about Wilson except from this grammar. Apparently working from the Department of Indian Affairs and Northern Development copy, which was undated, she states that the manual "was written around the turn of the century, as there is a word for railroad, but none for a car, telephone, or electric toothbrush" (ibid., p.15). She is off by a quarter of a century. She opines that she knows "what happened to Wilson, he got lonely. Years and years on the North Shore . . . " (ibid., p.16). In fact the manual was the work of a young missionary still driven by his evangelical religion before the years of his experience ripened after 1885. He had spent several years in southwestern Ontario before a fairly recent move to the north, to Sault Ste. Marie.

Jiles begins tongue in cheek with the mock revelation that "once in a great while a person is priviledged [sic] to find, on their own and unassisted by grants a true unknown Canadian Classic. Like most unknown Canadian Classics, no one reads them very much, and I feel that this one has not had the critical attention it deserves" (1976, 15).

Her satire depends on the cleaned-up ideal portrait of western culture portrayed by the white missionary as he tells his Native clientele to work hard, avoid drink and improper sex, and to attend church regularly: "Wilson does what the bureaucrats, the administrators, and the men of God have always done in the north and continue to do: present white society as unified and classless, made up of Hobbits and sturdy yeoman, solidly behind the Christian ethic, Protestant to the core" (ibid., 17).

Sex of course is avoided or mentioned indirectly in Wilson's grammar book, such as in the entry for menstruation where "the Reverend says stiffly, 'See Catamenia.' " Another target for Jiles' satire is the entry for the "adulterer" which translates as "one who knows strange women and an 'adulteress' is one who knows strange men" (ibid.). Jiles comments, "Reading through the dictionary section a person would be convinced that white people reproduce by nuclear fission, or budding, or sending out pseudopods" (ibid.). Here, surely, is the voice of the 1970s, newly liberated from sexual mores which broke down in the 1960s. "Reverend Wilson" certainly knew about sex as he was married and eventually sired a brood of eleven children. It seems hard for Jiles to empathize with the different social world of the evangelical Victorian missionary.

Such clergy persons were particularly keen to advance the official culture of ideals rather than the real culture of practice. To us today this will seem like hypocrisy. Jiles rhetorically asks what such a portrayal tells "the white reader" about ourselves. "That none of us ever touch a drop of liqueur. We think those who do will never enter heaven. We all live in great English houses that take three years to build, we are androids and never do IT, and babies are found in mailboxes, where they have been delivered. . . . People who work hard prosper and labour has its true reward. And we love that Great White Mother of us all who lives across the Great Water" (Ibid., p.17).

It is unlikely that such a satirical narrative would be written today. In the 1960s and 1970s Canada was in the midst of a massive rejection of previously accepted roles, statuses, traditions and conventions. The Christian churches certainly were, at least at first glance, among the victims of the 1960s ethos, although some may argue that in the long run a more prophetic role has reanimated them. At the time, however, the churches lost support and became easy targets for disturbers of the status quo. It is in this context, surely, that the construction of Paulette Jiles' narrative must be understood.

The assault on the values, norms and institutions of the dominant society in the late 1960s and early 1970s often was exhibited in the form of irony, satire, critique, and rejection. In sociology, for example, essays and books which attacked the reigning paradigm of structural functionalism became more than a cottage industry. If one looks at the position of French Canadians, women, Blacks, Native peoples, the student critique of Amerika, the spirit of the times was one of "total rejection." While critique became a guiding mode of expression, there was also a halting movement toward alternatives. For example, in the context of Native policy, salt was poured on the wounds by the development in the late 1960s of the new Trudeau government's agenda, the White Paper on Indian Policy, announced on 25 June 1969.[1] The response by First Nations peoples was a massive rejection of the policy and the clearer articulation of alternatives, in particular "an emphasis in the 1970s on Indian self-government" (Miller 1990, 235).

A Text From the 1980s
White academic scholarship also expressed a clear rejection of prior practice, and the use of the notion of "colonialism" as a pejorative term denoting the use of power to subdue Native peoples became common. An early example to take this approach is E. Palmer Patterson's *The Canadian Indian: A History Since 1500* (1972). Because he is critical of the new paradigm dealing with Native peoples, James A. Clifton is able to identify its elements. The 1960s, he suggests, "witnessed a sharp, sudden break from the earlier narrative structure" (1989, 3). The older "prominent storyline" until the 1950s had been to portray an Indian past "as a time of stable

cultures which strongly contrasted with a maladapted disorganized present"
which would terminate in assimilation (ibid., 3). These narratives were
"communicated in a dispassionate, neutral objective style" (ibid.).

The new narrative style emphasizes "continuity and persistence" rather
than "cultural loss and disorganization" for Native peoples. "The code
words in these new accounts are exploitation, oppression, colonialism,
liberation, self-determination, victimization, sovereignty, cultural pluralism, resistance and nationhood" (ibid.). The new task or role for scholars
also asserted a changed self-image for white scholars as "helpful commen-
tators" or "involved advocates" rather than supposedly neutral and detached scientific observers. In explaining this "sudden break" with earlier
preferred narrative styles, Clifton points to such factors as "The decline of
colonialism and the rise of new nation states throughout the world and to
the rise of ethnic awareness and civil and minority rights movements in the
old nations" (ibid., 4). An anthology of *Readings on Canadian Native
History* (*Out of the Background,* 1988) demonstrates some of these narrative changes in several ways. Firstly, the introduction and several of the
papers are concerned to portray Native people as "not merely . . . standing
on the stage" but as having had "active and decisive roles," and not just as
"bit players" but as having influence on the "development of the plot"
(Fisher and Coates 1988, 2). This new interpretation of active Native
peoples of the past is reinforced by "the growing assertiveness of Native
people themselves" (ibid., 1) in the present.

These movements of social thought were thus in the wind as I worked
on the text that became *A Victorian Missionary and Canadian Indian
Policy* (1988). Although the new narrative structure is prominent in this
text, published as it was in the late 1980s, part of it was written many years
before as a piece of research completed for my MA degree at Carleton
University. Much of the research was done between 1970 and 1973. However, the original MA thesis did not include the chapters which deal with
the ideas of self-government and cultural synthesis.

In contrast to Peter Moore's portrayal of Wilson as the missionary
priest taking up the cross and serving the Lord, the emphasis in my own
text is on presenting E.F. Wilson as a pioneer among whites regarding the
ideas of self-government and cultural synthesis and continuity. This text,
too, is an exemplary story but its reason for putting the spotlight on Wilson
is different. There is an undeniable "whiggish" or "presentist" tone in this
narrative. I write that "although he was heavily involved in a program for
cultural replacement, he did come to think seriously of and to explore
novel ideas for social change which depended on cultural synthesis and
autonomy. . . . A study of E.F. Wilson, then, becomes a necessity for a
clearer understanding of the development of Indian policy in Canada"

(Nock 1988, 157). This quotation is placed just after a paragraph in which I point out the fate of the White Paper of 1969 and "the growing realization in Canada that cultural replacement might not be the unchallenged boon that had been assumed before" (ibid.). Look, my book seems to say, here is a pioneer for ideas of Native autonomy and Native cultural control as opposed to assimilation. Let us study his experience and see if we can learn something of use for today when such ideas have been reborn. The book is written, then, not simply as an historical study. As I argue, "These are problems that bedevil Canadians to this day and, because this is so, Wilson's experience between 1868 and 1893 remains alive, fresh, and relevant. Perhaps when such problems and issues are finally resolved, Wilson will be seen simply as another figure of antiquarian or local interest. That day has not yet come. . . ." (ibid., 160).

This stress on Wilson as a pioneer of the ideas of self-government and cultural synthesis and persistence affected the construction of the narrative. For example, Wilson's period of service for the Church Missionary Society from 1868 to 1872 is seen in the text as an initial experiment of cultural synthesis as advocated by the Church Missionary Society director, Henry Venn. Later on the narrative investigates the major sources of Wilson's new thought, those being his intellectual relationships with Horatio Hale and Helen Hunt Jackson and his personal observation and interaction with Native peoples and nations, in particular the Cherokee of Oklahoma. The high point of the narrative is the discussion of "The Fair Play Papers" and their author-ship as it is in these papers that the arguments about self-government and Native cultural persistence are given the most thoughtful exposition. Shortly after this comes Wilson's disillusionment and resignation.

A reader who is able to compare my text and that of Moore will notice that after describing the building of the Shingwauk and its pedagogical system, I provide little detail about the controversies surrounding its con-trol, financing and expansion. This did not fit comfortably into my narra-tive and thus is largely excluded, whereas it is a major point of discussion for Peter Moore. Neither Moore nor I include lengthy sections on Wilson's life in British Columbia. His years there were spent a) as an Anglican clergyperson dealing with white settlers; b) as an orchard farmer; and c) as an author writing about the Bible. None of these pastimes fit comfortably into Moore's text which emphasizes Wilson as a "missionary priest" min-istering to needy Natives, nor into mine, dealing as it does with an exem-plary hero and pioneer of the themes of Native cultural synthesis and persistence. In fact Wilson's retirement, coming in the wake of the failure of a planned conference dealing with policy issues and alternatives for Native peoples (see Nock 1988, 145-146; and Nock 1982b) was something of an abrupt and unexpected departure. This issue is treated better in Peter

Moore's text where it is dealt within the context of the controversies and frustrations over the ongoing operation of the schools.

In terms of a mode of emplotment (to use Hayden White's term, I would suggest that "comedy" is the one most appropriate for my text. It must be remembered that comedy does not refer to riotous humour, but a situation in which "hope is held out for the temporary triumph of man over his world by the prospect of occasional *reconciliation* of the forces at play in the social and natural worlds. Such reconciliations are symbolized in the festive occasions which the Comic writer traditionally uses to terminate his dramatic accounts of change and transformation" (White 1973, 9).

Emplotment of my work as "romantic" is made untenable because at the outset I deny the purpose of the book is heroic character presentation. I reject the aim of traditional history as suggested by the late noted historian Donald Creighton, that its goal was "the elucidation of character . . . " (1972, 19). Rather the emphasis was on presenting a case study of different policies used by whites in their dealings with North America's Native peoples" (Nock 1988, 1). My work is not best seen as a tragedy where there are "no festive occasions except false or illusory ones." (White 1973, 9). In comedy the conflict between humans is seen not as irremediable but "in the long run, harmonizable with one another" (ibid., 9). In my text these moments of festivity and reconciliation are presented in the discussion of cultural synthesis and autonomy as more optimistic policy options than the long-running options of cultural replacement and assimilation. Thus my text leads up to the "festive occasion" of the discussion of The Fair Play Papers and also the influences on Wilson which led him to such an epiphany.

It is true that there is a certain sadness at the end of the book due in part to Wilson's retirement in some frustration from the impediments in his way and the fear that his ideas of "Indian self-government and the Native Indian church" would have "little chance . . . ever being realized at any rate in my own day" (Nock 1988, 5). However this ending cannot be said to represent tragedy in which the protagonist has challenged, and failed, against "inalterable and external" conditions (White 1973, 9). The appeal of *A Victorian Missionary and Canadian Indian Policy* is that modern readers know that the epoch of the last twenty years has revitalized those ideas and we have even seen at least limited implementation of them (although certainly not to the degree desired by Native organizations). Thus my text ends on an upbeat, despite the resignation of Wilson, as it points in the direction of new festive occasions in the 1970s and 1980s.

Modes of Ideological Implication
Each of the three texts contains what Hayden White calls modes of ideo-

logical implication (see page 102). The conservative mode is easiest to see in the 1950s text by Peter Moore. In the 1970s and 1980s, after the abolition of church-run residential schools, there was a marked rejection of them by both Natives and the dominant white society. This turn-around of attitudes has been rapid and massive and it may require an enormous change of our gestalt to remember or to create an image of a time, not so long ago, when the Christian churches received a great deal of respect in general, including for their mission of "westernizing" Native children into the ways of the dominant society. Thus Moore's references to the schools established by Wilson are positive. In the conclusion we read: "The Shingwauk and Wawanosh homes stand today as living witnesses to Wilson and his evangelistic zeal" (Moore 1959, 59). In the preface we read that the Shingwauk "stands today as a living witness to his dedicated ministry." Moore's criticism is not of the schools or the conduct of their personnel; but a shared feeling with the missionary of "a certain bitterness toward the Canadian people for their lack of interest" (ibid., 54).

In my own text, the mode of ideological implication is undoubtedly radical in the sense that the high point of Wilson's career is not seen as the establishment of the missionary schools, but the writing of the radical Fair Play Papers and the planning of an aborted conference. The merits of Native self-government and cultural synthesis were to be discussed as alternatives to the reigning orthodoxy of wardship leading to eventual incorporation into the dominant society and massive resocialization in terms of culture.

Some reviewers have pointed out that I put considerable emphasis on these ideas of self-government and cultural synthesis despite the consideration that this new point of view had little effect at this time, and in fact, was soon terminated by Wilson's resignation. John Webster Grant, author of a most important text on missionary-Native encounters (1984) takes this line in part when he comments, "What some may query is the importance of a few articles that seem to have had no effect on either church or government policies at the time and had been almost completely forgotten when change eventually came" (1990, 422). It is helpful to remember Hayden White's assertion that all texts are invested with moral, social and political implications. The author of this text, Nock, grew up in an Anglican clerical family in the academic climate of the late 1960s and early 1970s. He is not inclined to debunk religious practitioners root-and-branch, but neither can he simply endorse what to an earlier generation had seemed a self-evident boon. Emphasizing Wilson's intellectual "conversion" (as it is dubbed by Grant 1990, 421) allows Nock to underline that clergy, particularly Anglican clergy, had at least some insights that went beyond high Victorian ethnocentrism. Thus at the deepest levels of the text, there lurks a denominational apologetic purpose. However, I do not apologize for that purpose as we have seen that no text is a naive representation simply of fact.

Finally a word on the text of Paulette Jiles. One has to start with a recognition that Jiles' knowledge of Wilson is acknowledged to be incomplete. My own knowledge of Jiles is distinctly limited. But her text reveals a massive rejection of anything that characterizes the point of view of a nineteenth century Evangelical Protestant clergyman trying to resocialize the Native peoples. Thus Wilson is a "blathering sack of chloroform" who provides tidbits of "these embarrassing leftovers of the Protestant Ethic." The ideological mode of Wilson's language is interpreted as "not that of the poet, the visiting traveller, or even the thinker, but rather the language of the conqueror" (Jiles 1976, 15).

In terms of typifying Jiles according to the modes of ideological implication, it is obvious that hers is hardly a conservative analysis. Nor is its mode "liberal" in which change is sought in the form of adjustments and "fine tunings." I suspect the anarchist mode hits the mark most accurately. Underlining this text is an absolute sense of the integrity of Native society and people. It ends with her anecdote of approaching a Native leader (Chief Frank Stone of the Michipicoten Reserve) with some words taken from Wilson's "Ojibway grammar" only to be told that he (Wilson) had got it wrong. She concludes: "I decided the word best suiting my purposes in the dictionary was 'odeeko-wau-benaun —He, she, or it casts it aside,' and began to learn by ear, from the little kids" (ibid., 17). The implication is that programs for change of whatever stripe are misdirected without the closest possible connection with actual Native communities. This accords well with the anarchist tradition of stressing local community control unmediated by indirect layers of government.

Conclusion
In this chapter I have tried to point out the usefulness of postmodernist theory, as represented by Hayden White, and of the sociology of knowledge in coming to an understanding of three texts dealing with E.F. Wilson, the nineteenth century missionary, educator, anthropologist and social activist. The older positivistic conceptions which emphasize the role of the historian simply as a disinterested collector of external facts about the past fail. They fail because, as Hayden White tell us, our collection of "facts" will be determined by the mode of emplotment (and also the modes of argument and ideological implication) which affect the historian. One cannot write "ex nihilo," before pen gets to paper or fingers get to microcomputer; the need to construct an identifiable narrative will already have affected which facts are picked up as shiny gems

and which are rejected as unnecessary or irrelevant.

As we have also seen, the surrounding culture affects the modes of narrative construction employed. Michel Foucault, a guru of postmodernism, talked of the succession of "epistemes," or conventional understandings which shape discourse. Foucault suggests:

> It seemed to me that in certain empirical forms of knowledge like biology, political economy, psychiatry, medicine, etc. the rhythm of transformation doesn't follow the smooth continuist schemes of development which are normally accepted . . . . In a science like medicine, for example, up to the end of the eigtheenth century one has a certain type of discourse whose gradual transformation, within a period of twenty-five or thirty years, broke not only with the 'true' propositions which it had hitherto been possible to formulate, but also, more profoundly, with the ways of speaking and seeing, the whole ensemble of practices which served as supports for medical knowledge. These are not simply new discoveries, there is a whole new 'regime' in discourse and forms of knowledge. And all this happens in the space of a few years (1980, 111-112).

Thus it is that history has to be written over and over again; certainly each generation will see things differently, and it is likely that significant social variables will also affect narrative construction. Perhaps I may be permitted to end as comedians do with the bad news and the good news. The bad news is that historical research is like Sisyphus rolling up his or her boulder only to have it fall down and then to be condemned to repeat the effort. The good news is that a finite bedrock of fact on any one topic is unlikely to exhaust the subject as the same quarry of "fact" will over time and among different subcultures be reinterpreted on the basis of rather different principles of interpretation and narrative construction.

In this current analysis of the modes of emplotment and the ideological implications embedded in three texts dealing with the Victorian missionary, E.F. Wilson, we have seen how the selection of "fact" is effected by these factors. There is no portrait which stands as a definitive or final representation of this figure, nor can there be. What we have in the writing of history is an ongoing process of discourse and debate, and not the invocation of some sort of positivistic closure.

Note

[1] The White Paper suggested that the reason for the lack of Native peoples' development had been their special status under the Canadian law. The solution proposed was to terminate this special status by closing the Department of Indian Affairs and by Native people relating to governments "as individuals in precisely the way that other citizens did" (Miller 1990, 226).

Chapter Seven

Conclusion

This volume has sought to establish that certain traditions of positivistic epistemology need to be rejected for the simple reason that they provide an inadequate guide to interpreting texts. One of the results of a positivistic epistemology is the creation of an academic star-system without a proper critical apparatus provided to students and other colleagues. Most academic stars are created because of the feeling we have that someone has "got the goods" on a certain area of research. Even when we "know better," that is when we have read some post-positivistic accounts of knowledge, we get carried away into believing that someone has managed to quarry a set of facts which better represent the "real world." Part of this is due, I am sure, to an entrenched "presentism" among academics. There is a largely unspoken feeling that what is recent is better, and what is older is out-of-date and inadequate. Academics share in the modern myth of progress that history is debunked and useless, a preserve of old and quaint notions. We are enjoined by some to forget our progenitors because new and better methods of eliciting "fact" means that there is a built-in obsolescence to knowledge. An experience which comes to mind from some years ago is a professor who ignored conservative conflict theorists such as Pareto and Michels in a political studies course in favour of consensus-oriented structural functionalists, because he felt the former were out-of-date compared to David Easton and Talcott Parsons.

As far as the creation of "stars" is concerned, there are a number of drawbacks. Sociologists, in my experience, tend to take the data (especially when in the form of statistics) of other sociologists "for granted" without adequate consideration of the perceptions and perspectives engaged, or of hermeneutic principles of interpretation. With all the critical writing over the years since about 1975 which relates to John Porter, it is a matter of some amazement to me to find *The Vertical Mosaic* warmly praised as late as 1987 as "one of the best works on social stratification in Canada" (Grabb 1987, 159). I wince to think of students in the late 1980s being directed to a view of Canada that may have been adequate in the 1940s and 1950s but which even at its original date of publication contained important methodological and philosophical problems (Ogmundson 1990; Brym with Fox 1989).

I should like to add that my aim here is *not* to single out any one author for such faults. I can cite my own somewhat breathless endorsement of Rodney Stark and W.S. Bainbridge's tome *The Future of Religion* (1985) as "bold new research" (Nock 1986, 309). My point is that what prompts us to make such endorsements is frequently an uncritical acceptance of the "empirical data" which is presented as a "realist" representation of "the real world."

There are certain pressures on us which lead us in such uncritical directions. My experience is that the students of the 1980s and 1990s want to be taught something that will inform them about the external world. They want answers which are pithy and straight-forward. They are not comfortable with stories which get complicated with the sociological observer's cultural or perceptual influences. It seems that most under-graduates are innately tied to a positivistic conception of knowledge. No doubt a good deal of the reason for this lies in the hands of instructors. I am convinced that one of the reasons why much of the tabular data from John Porter (and his heirs such as Wallace Clement and Denis Olsen) has remained popular in textbooks for so long has been that it is easy to teach. One puts numbers up on the blackboard or overhead projector which relate to ethnicity, religion and class, and then both instructor and student can move on to the next issue convinced that they have covered those topics. Numbers have a tendency to dispel argument. A mathematician, Neal Koblitz, has identified some uses of the subject in the social sciences. He writes:

> In some quarters, invoking an equation or statistic can be even more persuasive than citing a well-known authority. . . . An argument which would be quickly disputed if stated in plain English will often acquire some momentum if accompanied by numbers and formulas, regardless of whether or not they are relevant or accurate. Who can argue with an equation? An equation is always exact, indisputable. Challenging someone who can support his claim with an equation is as pointless as arguing with your high school math teacher (cited in Sykes 1988, 210).

It is my partially intuitive observation that articles by Canadian sociologists most cited in the *Social Science Citation Index* are those which contain statistics as a key source of data and which are capable of easy summary.

Another source of this problematic reliance on numbers is the increasing orientation of our universities toward research rather than scholarship. By research I mean work in the social sciences and humanities which presupposes the positivistic methods of the natural sciences and a reliance on large research grants usually involving teams of investigators "led" by a faculty member and involving paid employees as researchers. In recent years in Canadian universities, there has been increased pressure to acquire funding either from NSRC or SSHRC (large federally-supported funding agencies for the natural sciences and social sciences respectively). This is because of a new formula applied several years ago by SSHRC which ties local internal university funding grants to research money awarded externally by SSHRC in "research competitions." In addition, universities are often ranked now by the percentage of "SSHRC and NSERC-eligible faculty" (to use an actual phrase) to hold grants. The implication of all this is that faculty who do not hold such grants or enter such competitions are not doing anything of value. One result of such pressure on arts faculties has been a rapid increase in SSHRC applications. NSRC already awards money to a *majority* of applicants, whereas SSHRC has traditionally funded less than 40 percent of applicants, a percentage which is now going down because of the flood of new applicants.

This is not to say that funding of research, where necessary, is a waste. However the new situation as it exists is informed by two realities: many persons in the humanities and social sciences are capable of doing valuable research and scholarly writing without the need for funding, or with the need for only minor grants, yet there is increased pressure to apply for research grants. Universities advise applicants to ask for the largest grant possible and to over-estimate costs. University faculty are creative and, no doubt, will find ways to apply for grants even when they are unnecessary and a waste of public money. The deeper tragedy of this situation is that the social sciences and humanities increasingly come to resemble the natural sciences, even where it is not appropriate. Any applicant for funding to SSHRC using the forms supplied in the 1980s could not but be impressed with how oriented it was to a natural science rather than social science or humanities gestalt. The ideal grant application presumed that the researcher had an hypothesis pre-established that called for "testing" which would depend on the use of assistants and research employees. Such assumptions replicate the positivistic methodology and philosophy of the natural sciences and seem sadly out of step with the methods of many of the social sciences and humanities. One is reminded by George Grant, arguably the most distinguished "humanist" and even, despite himself, social scientist produced in Canada, "The strange event is this: the more the humanities have gained wealth and prestige by taking on the language and methods of the progressive sciences, the less significance they have in the society they inhabit" (1986, 100).

Finally, university faculty must ask themselves why so much attachment to the positivistic conception remains among their own ranks. I feel sure that this has something to do with an existential problem: the desire for immortality. Consciously or not, even while voicing cynical remarks, most faculty feel or hope that through publications they can establish a type of memory than can survive their death.

However the memory they wish to preserve is that of the positivistic researcher who "just finds out the facts" about external reality. To suggest that our analyses are affected by our perceptions and by our subcultural attachments is, for many, to disturb the value of what we have produced. We wish to be known for the "definitive" analysis of this or that subject, even when we know, in our better judgement, that there is no such thing.

If I am correct, then there exist many reasons why positivistic assumptions remain powerful despite the impact of works such as Thomas Kuhn's *The Structure of Scientific Revolutions* and other developments. Moreover there is some reason to doubt that the influence of post-positivistic epistemology will survive healthily into the next twenty years. The 1960s and 1970s, afterall, were decades of radicalism which led into a subsequent period of cynicism, doubt and negativity on a grand scale.

Some ideological trends, such as the alleged end of communism, have given many a new smugness in the moral and material superiority of industrial-capitalism. There is a new feeling unmatched since the 1950s that the West and its general framework is "right." We may ask if the vision of Margaret Thatcher is not the emerging one of the 1990s. It is known that Thatcher started out her career as a natural scientist before turning to law, and it is a little difficult to imagine that, with her sharp and abrupt judgements, she entertains much affection for the idea of post-positivistic epistemology.

And yet it is my contention (and that of Barnes and Bloor) that "far from being a threat to the scientific understanding of forms of knowledge, relativism is required by it" (1982, 21). Barnes and Bloor go on to suggest that "it is those who oppose relativism, and who grant certain forms of knowledge a privileged status, who pose the real threat to a scientific understanding of knowledge and cognition" (ibid., 22). As they suggest, there are "no context-free or super-cultural norms of rationality" (ibid, 27). Those who believe there are these norms may sleep well, convinced they have uncovered some form of absolute truth. However, they risk confusing parochialism with verisimilitude and prejudgement with veracity.

References

Abercrombie, Nicholas. 1980. *Class, Structure, and Knowledge*. New York, New York University Press.

Agger, Ben. 1991. "Critical Theory, Poststructuralism, Postmodernism: Their Sociological Relevance" *Annual Review of Sociology*, vol. 17, edited by W. Richard Scott and Judith Blake. Palo Alto, CA, Annual Reviews.

American Sociological Association. 1989. *Guide to Graduate Departments of Sociology*. Washington, D.C., ASA

Aronowitz, Stanley. 1988. *Science as Power: Discourse and Ideology in Modern Society*. Minneapolis, University of Minnesota Press.

Assheton-Smith, Marilyn. 1979. "John Porter's Sociology: A Theoretical Basis for Canadian Education" *Canadian Journal of Education*, vol. 4, no. 2, pp. 43-54.

Association of Commonwealth Universities. 1988. *Commonwealth Universities Yearbook 1988*, vol. 2. London, A.C.U.

Bain, Read. 1926. "Trends in American Sociology" *Social Forces*, vol. 5, pp. 413-422.

Bannister, Robert C. 1987. *Sociology and Scientism: The American Quest for Objectivity*. Chapel Hill and London, University of North Carolina Press.

Barnes, Barry. 1974. *Scientific Knowledge and Sociological Theory*. London, Routledge and Kegan Paul.

Barnes, Barry. 1977. *Interests and the Growth of Knowledge*. London, Routledge and Kegan Paul.

Barnes, Barry and David Bloor. 1982. "Relativism, Rationalism and the Sociology of Knowledge" in Martin Hollis and Steven Lukes, eds., *Rationality and Relativism*, Oxford, Basil Blackwell.

Baum, Gregory. 1977. *Truth Beyond Relativism: Karl Mannheim's Sociology of Knowledge*. Milwaukee, Marquette University Press.

Bellah, Robert N. 1957. *Tokugawa Religion*. New York, Free Press.

Bellah, Robert N. 1964. "Research Chronicle: Tokugawa Religion" in Phillip E. Hammond, ed., *Sociologists at Work*. New York, Basic Books.

Berger Carl. 1976. *The Writing of Canadian History: Aspects of English-Canadian Historical Writing: 1900-1970*. Toronto, Oxford University Press.

Berkowitz, S.D. 1984. "Models, Myths and Social Realities: A Brief Introduction to Sociology in Canada" in S.D. Berkowitz, ed., *Models and Myths in Canadian Sociology*. Toronto, Butterworths.

Bernard, L.L. 1909. "The Teaching of Sociology in the United States" *American Journal of Sociology*, vol. 15, no. 2, pp. 164-213.

Bibby, Reginald W. 1987. *Fragmented Gods: The Poverty and Potential of Religion in Canada*. Toronto, Irwin Publishing.

Black, Edwin R. 1974. "The Fractured Mosaic: John Porter Revisited" *Canadian Public Administration*, no. 17, pp. 640-653.

Bloor, David. 1976. *Knowledge and Social Imagery*. London, Routledge and Kegan Paul.

Blumer, Herbert. 1931. "Science Without Concepts" *American Journal of Sociology*, vol. 36, no. 4, pp. 515-533.

Brooks, Stephen and Alain G. Gagnon. 1989. *Social Scientists and Politics in Canada: Between Clerisy and Vanguard*. Montreal, McGill-Queens University Press.

Brunet, Michel. 1954. *Canadians et Canadiens*. Montreal, Fides.

Brunet, Michel. 1964. *La Présence Anglaise et les Canadiens: Etudes sur l'histoire et la pensée des deux Canadas*. Montreal, Beauchemin.

Brym, Robert J. 1984. "Social Movements and Third Parties" in S.D. Berkowitz, ed., *Models and Myths in Canadian Sociology*. Toronto, Butterworths.

Brym, Robert J. 1986. "Anglo-Canadian Sociology" *Current Sociology*, vol. 34, no. 1, Spring, pp. 1-152.

Brym, Robert J. 1986. *Regionalism in Canada*. Toronto, Irwin Publishing.

Brym. Robert J. with Bonnie J. Fox. 1989. *From Culture to Power: The Sociology of English Canada*. Toronto, Oxford University Press.

Brym, Robert J. and R. James Sacouman. 1979. *Underdevelopment and Social Movements in Atlantic Canada*. Toronto, New Hogtown Press.

Bulmer, Martin. 1984. *The Chicago School of Sociology*. Chicago, University of Chicago Press.

Campbell, Douglas F. 1983. *Beginnings: Essays on the History of Canadian Sociology*. Port Credit, The Scribblers' Press.

Careless, J.M.S. 1948. "The Toronto Globe and Agrarian Radicalism, 1850-1867" *The Canadian Historical Review*, vol. XXIX, no. 1.

Carr, E. H.1961.*What is History?* London, Macmillan.

Carrington, P. 1963. *The Anglican Church in Canada*. Toronto, Collins.

CJS. 1989. Cumulative Index 1974-1988.*The Canadian Journal of Sociology*.

Clark, S. Delbert. 1932a. "Letters to the editor" *Lloydminster Times*, 14 January; 9, 11, 16, 18 February; 24, 29 March; 28 July; 18 August; 3, 17 November; 15, 22 December.

Clark, S. Delbert. 1932b. "The United Farmers of Alberta" *Canadian Forum*, XIII, October, pp. 7-8.

Clark, S. Delbert. 1933. "Letters to the editor" *Lloydminster Times*, 27 April 1933; 18 May.

Clark, S.D. 1938. "The Canadian Manufactuers' Association: A Political Pressure Group" *Canadian Journal of Economics and Political Science*, no. iv, pp. 505-523.

Clark, S.D. 1939. "The Canadian Manufacturers' Association and the Tariff" *Canada Journal of Economics and Political Science*, no. v, pp. 19-39.

Clark, S.D. 1942. *The Social Development of Canada*, Toronto, University of Toronto Press.

Clark, S.D. 1948. *Church and Sect in Canada*, Toronto, University of Toronto Press.

Clark, S.D. 1953. "Foreword" in C.B. Macpherson, *Democracy in Alberta: Social*

Credit and the Party System. Toronto, University of Toronto Press.

Clark, S.D. 1959. *Movements of Political Protest in Canada 1640-1840*, Toronto, University of Toronto Press.

Clark, S.D. 1962. *The Developing Canadian Community*, Toronto, University of Toronto Press.

Clark, S.D. 1976a. *Canadian Society in Historical Perspective*, Toronto, McGraw-Hill Ryerson.

Clark, S.D. 1976b. *The Canadian Society and the Issue of Multi-culturalism*, Saskatoon, University of Saskatchewan Sorokin.

Clark, S.D. 1979. "The Changing Image of Sociology in English-Speaking Canada" *The Canadian Journal of Sociology*, no. iv, pp. 393-403.

Clarkson, Stephen. 1985. *Canada and the Reagan Challenge: Crisis and Adjustment, 1981-85.* Toronto, James Lorimer.

Clement, Wallace. 1980. "Searching for Equality: The Sociology of John Porter" *Canadian Journal of Political and Social Theory*, vol. 4, no. 2, Spring-Summer, pp. 97-114.

Clifton, James A. 1989. *Being and Becoming Indian: Biographical Studies of North American Frontiers.* Chicago, The Dorsey Press.

Cole, Jonathan R. and Stephen Cole. 1971. "Measuring the Quality of Sociological Research: Problems in the Use of the Science Citation Index" *The American Sociologist*, vol. 6, no. 2.

Cole, Jonathan R. and Stephen Cole. 1973. *Social Stratification in Science.* Chicago, University of Chicago Press.

Conway, J.F. 1978. "Populism in the U.S.. Russia and Canada: Explaining the Roots of Canada's Third Parties" *The Canadian Journal of Political Science*, no. 11, pp. 99-124.

Conway, J.F. 1979. "The Prairie Populist Resistance to the National Policy: Some Reconsiderations" *Journal of Canadian Studies*, no. xiv, pp. 77-91.

Conway, J.F. 1983a. Review of Harry H. Hiller, "Society and Change: S.D. Clark and Development of Canadian Sociology" *Canadian Journal of Political Science*, no. xvi, pp. 366-367.

Conway, J.F. 1983b. *The West: The History of a Region in Confederation.* Toronto, James Lorimer.

Cook, Ramsay. 1966. *Canada and the French-Canadian Question.* Toronto, Macmillan.

Cook, Ramsay. 1971. *The Maple Leaf Forever: Essays on Nationalism and Politics in Canada.* Toronto, Macmillan.

Crane, Diana. 1965. "Scientists at Major and Minor Universities: A Study of Production and Recognition" *American Sociological Review*, vol. 30, no. 5, pp. 699-714.

Crane, Diana. 1967. "The Gatekeepers of Science: Some Factors Affecting the Selection of Articles for Scientific Journals" *The American Sociologist*, vol. 12, no. 4, pp. 194-201.

Creighton, Donald.1972. "The Economic Background of the Rebellions of 1837" in *Towards the Discovery of Canada: Selected Essays*, Toronto, Macmillan.

Cross, Michael. 1970. *The Frontier Thesis and the Canadas.* Toronto, Copp Clark.

Crothers, Charles. 1984. "Patterns of Regional Social Differences in New Zealand" *The Australian and New Zealand Journal of Sociology*, vol. 20, no. 3, pp. 365-376.

Crothers, Charles. 1987. *Robert K. Merton.* London, Tavistock.

CRSA. 1986. Index/Index 1964-1984. *The Canadian Review of Sociology and Anthropology*. Toronto, University of Toronto Press.

Crysdale, S. and J-P. Montminy. 1974. *Religion in Canada, 1945-1972*. Quebec, Les Presses de l'Université Laval.

Curtis, James and Lorne Teppermen. eds. 1990. *Images of Canada: The Sociological Tradition*, Scarborough, Prentice Hall.

Cuttell, Colin. 1988. *Philip Carrington: Pastor, Prophet, Poet*. Toronto, Anglican Book Centre.

Davis, Arthur K. 1971. "Canadian Society and History as Hinterland versus Metropolis" in Richard J. Ossenbeg, ed., *Canadian Society: Pluralism, Change and Conflict*. Scarborough, Prentice Hall.

Davis, Arthur K. 1978. "The Failure of American Import Sociology in Anglophone Canada" in R.W. Nelsen and D.A. Nock, eds., *Reading, Writing and Riches in Education and the Socio-Economic Order in North America*. Toronto, Between the Lines.

Deegan, Mary Jo. 1989. *Jane Addams and the Men of the Chicago School, 1892-1918*. New Brunswick, NJ, Transaction Books.

Dunham, Aileen. 1963. *Political Unrest in Upper Canada 1815-1836*. First published in 1927. Toronto, McClelland and Stewart.

Eliade, Mircea. 1963. *Myth and Reality*. New York, Harper and Row.

Ellwood, Charles. 1923-1924. "Scientific Methods of Studying Human Society" *The Journal of Social Forces*, no. 2, pp. 328-332.

Fisher, Robin and Kenneth Coates, eds. 1988. *Out of the Background: Readings in Canadian Native History*. Toronto, Copp Clark Pitman Ltd.

Fleck, Ludwik. 1979. *Genesis and Development of a Scientific Fact*. First published 1935. Chicago, University of Chicago.

Foucault, Michel. 1980. *Power/Knowledge: Selected Interviews and Other Writings, 1972-1977*. Colin Gordon, ed. New York, Pantheon Books.

Francis, R. Douglas. 1986. *Frank H. Underhill: Intellectual Provocateur*. Toronto, University of Toronto Press.

Giddings, Franklin H. 1901. *Inductive Sociology*. New York, Macmillan.

Giddings, Franklin H. 1922. "The Measurement of Social Forces" *The Journal of Social Forces*, vol. 1, no. 1, pp. 1-6.

Giddings, Franklin H. 1923. "The Scientific Scrutiny of Societal Facts" *The Journal of Social Forces*. vol. 1, no. 5, pp. 509-513.

Gittings, Gary, ed. 1980. *Paradigms and Revolutions: Appraisals and Applications of Thomas Kuhn's Philosophy of Science*. Notre Dame and London, University of Notre Dame Press.

Grabb, Edward G. 1987. "Social Stratification" in James J. Teevan, ed., *Basic Sociology: A Canadian Introduction*. Scarborough, Prentice Hall.

Grant, George. 1986. *Technology and Justice*. Toronto, Anansi.

Grant, John Webster. 1984. *Moon of Wintertime: Missionaries and the Indians of Canada in Encounter since 1534*. Toronto, University of Toronto Press.

Grant, John Webster. 1990. "Review of a Victorian Missionary and Canadian Indian Policy" *Church History*, vol. 59, no. 3, September, pp. 421-422.

Hammer, Heather-Jo. 1983-84. *Mature Dependency: The Effects of American Direct Investment on Canadian Economic Growth*. PhD dissertation, University of Alberta.

Hammer, Heather-Jo and John W. Gartrell. 1986. "American Penetration and Canadian Development: A Case Study of Mature Development" *American Sociological Review*, no. 51, pp. 201-213.

Harrison, Deborah. 1981. *The Limits of Liberalism: the Making of Canadian Sociology*. Montreal, Black Rose Books.

Harrison, Deborah. 1983. "The Limits of Liberalism in Canadian Sociology: Some Notes on S.D. Clark" *The Canadian Review of Sociology and Anthropology*, no. xx, pp. 150-166.

Harvey, Lee. 1987. *Myths of the Chicago School of Sociology*. Aldershot, UK, Aveburg.

Heap, James L., ed., 1974. *Everybody's Canada: The Vertical Mosaic Reviewed and Re-examined*. Toronto, Burns and MacEachern Limited.

Helmes-Hayes, Richard C. 1986. "Images of Inequality in Early Canadian Sociology, 1900-1965." Paper delivered at the annual meeting of the Ontario Anthropology and Sociology Association, Waterloo, Ontario.

Helmes-Hayes, R., ed. 1988. *A Quarter-Century of Sociology at the University of Toronto 1963-1988*. Toronto, Canadian Scholars' Press.

Herman, Kathleen, ed. 1986. *1986-87 Guide to Departments: Sociology, Anthropology, Archaeology in Universities and Museums in Canada*. Canadian Sociology and Anthropology Association and Canadian Ethnology Society.

Herman, Kathleen and Peter Carstens, eds. *1978-79 Guide to Departments: Sociology, Anthropology, Archaeology in Universities and Museums in Canada*. Ottawa, Canadian Sociology and Anthropology Association and Canadian Ethnology Society.

Hiller, Harry H. 1976. "The Sociology of Religion in the Canadian Context" in G.N. Ramu and S.D. Johnson, eds. *Introduction to Canadian Society: Sociological Analysis*. Toronto, Macmillan.

Hiller, Harry H. 1977. "Internal Party Resolution and Third Party Emergence" *The Canadian Journal of Sociology*, no. 2, pp. 55-75.

Hiller, Harry H. 1979. "The Canadian Sociology Movement: Analysis and Assessment" *The Canadian Journal of Sociology*, no. iv, pp. 125-150.

Hiller, Harry H. 1982. *Society and Change: S.D. Clark and the Development of Canadian Sociology*. Toronto, University of Toronto Press.

Hiller, Harry H. 1986. *Canadian Society: A Macroanalysis*. Scarborough, Prentice-Hall.

Hofley, John R. 1981. "John Porter: His Analysis of Class and His Contribution to Canadian Sociology" *The Canadian Review of Sociology and Anthropology*, vol. 18, no. 15, pp. 595-606.

Horn, Michiel. 1980. *The League for Social Reconstruction: Intellectual Origins of the Democratic Left in Canada 1930-1942*. Toronto, University of Toronto Press.

Horowitz, Gad. 1974. "Creative Politics, Mosaics and Identity" in Heap, ed., *Everybody's Canada*. Toronto, Burns and MacEachern.

Horowitz, Irving L. 1974. "The Vertical Mosaic: A Review" in Heap, ed., *Everybody's Canada*. Toronto, Burns and MacEachern.

Hughes, E.C. 1943. *French Canada in Transition*. Chicago, University of Chicago Press.

Irvine, William. 1920. *The Farmer in Politics*. Toronto, McClelland and Stewart.

Janowitz, Morris. 1970. "Introduction" in R.E. Park and E.W. Burgess, *Introduction to the Science of Society*. Chicago, University of Chicago Press.

Jaques Cattell Press. 1978. *American Men and Women of Science: Social and Behavioral Sciences*, 13th edition. New York, R.R. Bowker Company

Jiles, Paulette. 1976. "Reverend Wilson and the Ojibway Grammar" *This Magazine*, vol. 10, no. 1, February-March, pp. 15-17.

Kecskemeti, Paul, ed. 1959. "Introduction" *Essays on the Sociology of Knowledge*. London, Routledge and Kegan Paul.

Kilbourn, William M. 1965. "The Writing of Canadian History" in Carl F. Klinck, ed., *Literary History of Canada*. Toronto, University of Toronto Press.

Kuhn, Thomas, S. 1957. *The Copernician Revolution*. Cambridge, MA, Harvard University.

Kuhn, Thomas S. 1970. *The Structure of Scientific Revolutions*. First published in 1962. Chicago, University of Chicago Press.

Kuhn, Thomas S. 1977. *The Essential Tension: Selected Studies in Scientific Tradition*. Chicago, University of Chicago Press.

Laycock, David. 1990. *Populism and Democratic Thought in the Canadian Prairies 1910 to 1945*. Toronto, University of Toronto Press.

Lepenies, Wolf. 1988. *Between Literature and Science: The Rise of Sociology*. Cambridge, Cambridge University Press.

Lindsey, Charles. 1862. *The Life and Times of Wm. Lyon Mackenzie*. Toronto, C.W., P.R.

Lindsey, Charles. 1909. *William Lyon Mackenzie*. Toronto, Morang.

Lipset, S.M. 1963. *The First New Nation: The United States in Historical and Comparative Perspective*. New York, Basic Books.

Lipset, S.M. 1969. "From Socialism to Sociology" in I.L. Horowitz, ed. *Sociological Self-Images: A Collective Portrait*. Beverly Hills, Sage.

Lundberg, George A. 1926-1927. "Case Work and the Statistical Method" *Social Forces*, no. 5, pp. 61-65.

Mann, W.E. 1955. *Sect, Cult and Church in Alberta*. Toronto, University of Toronto.

Mannheim, Karl. 1936. *Ideology and Utopia*. New York, Harcourt, Brace, and World.

Marchak, Patricia. 1986. "The Rise and Fall of the Peripheral State: The Case of British Columbia" in Robert J. Brym, ed. *Regionalism in Canada*, Toronto, Irwin Publishing.

Mardiros, Anthony. 1979. *William Irvine: The Life of a Prairie Radical*. Toronto, James Lorimer.

Martin, Chester. 1929. *Empire and Commonweath: Studies in Governance and Self-Government in Canada*. Oxford, Clarendon Press.

Matthews, Fred H. 1977. *Quest For an American Sociology: Robert E. Park and the Chicago School*. Montreal, McGill-Queen's University Press.

McCrorie, James N. 1971. "Change and Paradox in Agrarian Social Movements" in Richard J. Ossenberg, ed., *Canadian Society*. Scarborough, Prentice Hall.

McCrorie, James N. 1979. *Changing Times: Relevant Theory*. Saskatoon, University of Saskatchewan Sorokin.

McKillop, A.B. 1979. *A Disciplined Intelligence: Critical Inquiry and Canadian*

Thought in the Victorian Era. Montreal, McGill-Queen's University Press.

Merton, Robert K. 1968. "The Matthew Effect in Science" *Science*, no. 159, January-March, pp. 56-63.

Merton, Robert K. 1973.*The Sociology of Science.* Chicago, University of Chicago Press. Reprint of Merton, 1968.

Miller, J.R. 1990. *Skyscrapers hide the heavens: A History of Indian-White Relations in Canada.* Toronto, University of Toronto Press.

Mol, Hans. 1985. *Faith and Fragility: Religion and Identity in Canada.* Burlington, Ontario, Trinity Press.

Moore, Peter B. 1959. *Edward Francis Wilson: Missionary to the Ojibway Indians.* London, Ont.: Huron College thesis in partial fulfillment of the requirements for the degree of Bachelor of Theology.

Morton, W.L. 1960. "Review of Movements of Political Protest in Canada" *The Canadian Historical Review*, vol. 41, no. 3, September, pp. 243-5.

Mulkay, Michael. 1983. *Science and the Sociology of Knowledge.* London, George Allen and Unwin.

Mullins, Nicholas C. 1973. *Theories and Theory Groups in Contemporary American Sociology.* New York, Harper and Row.

Murphy, John W. 1988. "Making Sense of Post-Modern Sociology" *The British Journal of Sociology*, vol. 39, no. 4 pp. 600-614.

Nettler, Gwynn.1970. *Explanations.* New York, McGraw-Hill.

Nock, David A. 1973. "E.F. Wilson—The Founder and First Principal of Shingwauk" *Algoma Anglican*, vol. 17, no. 1, January, p.3.

Nock, David A. 1979. "Anglican Bishops and Indigenity" *Studies in Religion/ Sciences Religieuses*, vol. 8, no. 1, pp. 47-55.

Nock, David A. 1981. "The Anglican Episcopate and Changing Conceptions of Canadian Identity" *Canadian Review of Studies in Nationalism*, vol. 8, no. 1, Spring, pp. 85-99.

Nock, David A. 1982a. "Patriotism and Patriarchs: Anglican Archbishops and Canadianization" *Canadian Ethnic Studies*, vol. 14, no. 3, pp. 79-94.

Nock, David A. 1982b. "The Indian Conference that Never Was" *Ontario Indian*, vol. 5, no. 2, February, pp. 39, 42, 43, 45.

Nock, David A. 1983. "S.D. Clark in the Context of Canadian Sociology" *Canadian Journal of Sociology*, no. viii, pp. 79-97.

Nock, David A. 1986. "Religion" in K. Ishwaran, ed., *Sociology: An Introduction.* Don Mills, Ontario, Addison-Wesley Publishers.

Nock, David A. 1988. *A Victorian Missionary and Canadian Indian Policy: Cultural Synthesis vs. Cultural Replacement.* Waterloo, Wilfrid Laurier University Press.

Nock, D.A. and R.W. Nelsen. 1982. "Science, Ideology and 'Reading, Writing and Riches'" *Journal of Educational Thought*, no. xvi, pp. 73-88.

Novick, Peter. 1988. *That Noble Dream: "The Objectivity Question" and the American Historical Profession.* Cambridge, Cambridge University Press.

Ogburn, William F. 1934. "Trends in Social Science", Reprinted (1964) in *On Culture and Social Change: Selected Papers.* Chicago, University of Chicago Press.

Ogmundson, R. 1980. "Toward Study of the endangered Species Known as the Anglophone Canadian" *The Canadian Journal of Sociology*, vol. 5, no. 1, pp. 1-12.

Ogmundson, R. 1990. "Perspective on the Class and Ethnic Origins of Canadian Elites: A Methodological Critique of the Porter/Clement/Olsen Tradition" *The Canadian Journal of Sociology*, vol. 15, no. 2, Spring, pp. 165-177.

Olsen, Dennis. 1981. "Power, Elites, and Society"*The Canadian Review of Sociology and Anthropology*, vol. 18, no. 5, December, pp. 607-614.

Ormsby, W.G. 1960. "Review of Movements of Political Protest in Canada" *Queen's Quarterly*, vol. 67, no. 1, Spring, pp. 129-130.

Ossenberg, Richard J. ed. 1971. *Canadian Society's Pluralism, Change and Conflict*. Scarborough, Prentice Hall.

O'Toole, Roger. 1984. "Some Good Purpose: Notes on Religion and Political Culture in Canada" in S.D. Berkowitz, ed., *Models and Myths in Canadian Sociology*. Toronto, Butterworths.

O'Toole, Roger. 1985. "Society, the Sacred and the Secular: Sociological Observations on the Changing Role of Religion in Canadian Culture" in William Westfall, et al., *Canadian Issues—Themes Canadiens*, vol.viii. Ottawa, The Association for Canadian Studies.

Ouellet, Fernand. 1980. *Lower Canada, 1791-1840: Social Change and Nationalism*. Toronto, McClelland and Stewart.

Park, Robert E. and Ernest W. Burgess. 1970. *Introduction to the Science of Society*. First published in 1926. Chicago, University of Chicago Press.

Pelz, Werner. 1974. *The Scope of Understanding in Sociology*. London, Routledge and Kegan Paul.

Penlington, Norman, ed. 1971. *On Canada: Essays in Honour of Frank H. Underhill*. Toronto, University of Toronto Press.

Porter, John. 1965.*The Vertical Mosaic: An Analysis of Social Class and Power in Canada*. Toronto, University of Toronto Press.

Porter, John. 1968. "The Future of Upward Mobility" *American Sociological Review*, vol. 33, no. 1 February, pp. 5-19.

Porter, John. 1975. "Foreword" in W. Clement, *The Canadian Corporate Elite: An Analysis of Economic Power*. Toronto, McClelland and Stewart.

Porter, John. 1979. "Canadian Character in the Twentieth Century" *The Measure of Canadian Society: Education, Equality, and Opportunity*. Toronto, Gage.

Porter, Marion. 1981. "John Porter and Education: Technical Functionalist or Conflict Theorist" *The Canadian Review of Sociology and Anthropology*, vol. 18, no. 5, pp. 627-638.

Porter, Marion. 1988. "John Porter" *Society-Société*, vol. 12, no. 2, May, pp. 1-5.

Poster, Mark. 1984. *Foucault, Marxism and History*. London, Basil Blackwell.

Read, Colin. 1982. *The Rise in Western Upper Canada, 1837-8: The Duncombe Revolt and After*. Toronto, University of Toronto Press.

Rich, Harvey. 1976. "The Vertical Mosaic Revisited: Toward a Macro-Sociology of Canada" *Journal of Canadian Studies*, vol. 11, no. 1, February, pp. 14-31.

Rifkin, Jeremy. 1984. *Algeny: A New Word—A New World*. Harmondsworth, UK, Penguin Books.

Robin, Martin. 1974. "The Vertical Mosaic Reviewed" in Heap, ed., *Everybody's Canada*. Toronto, Burns and MacEachern.

Roper, Henry. 1988. "The Anglican Episcopate in Canada: An Historical Perspective" *Anglican and Episcopal History*, vol. LVII, no. 3, September, pp. 255-271.

Sacouman, R. James. 1983. "Regional Uneven Development, Regionalism and Struggle" J. Paul Grayson, ed., *Introduction to Sociology: An Alternate Approach*. Toronto, Gage.

Saram, P.A. 1986. "Contributions to Basic Sociology: A Canadian Appreciation" Paper presented at the annual meetings of the Western Association of Sociology and Anthropology, Thunder Bay, Ontario.

Sheridan, Alan. 1980. *Michel Foucault: The Will to Truth*. London, Tavistock.

Shore, Marlene. 1987. *The Science of Social Redemption: McGill, the Chicago School, and the Origins of Social Research in Canada*. Toronto, University of Toronto Press.

Silver, Arthur. 1983. "Review of F. Ouellet, Lower Canada, 1791-1840" *The Canadian Review of Sociology and Anthropology*, no. xx, pp. 507-509.

Sklair, Leslie. 1973. *Organized Knowledge*. St. Albans, Paladin.

Smith, Dusky Lee. 1983. "Review of D. Harrison, The Limits of Liberalism" *The Canadian Review of Sociology and Anthropology*, no. xx, pp. 359-360.

Stebbins, Robert A. 1990. *Sociology: The Study of Society*, 2nd edition. New York, Harper and Row.

Stehr, Nico and V. Meja. 1984. *Society and Knowledge*. New Brunswick, NJ., Transaction Books.

Storey, Norah. 1967. *The Oxford Companion to Canadian History and Literature*. Toronto, Oxford University Press.

Straus, Murray A. and David J. Radel.1969. "Eminence, Productivity, and Power of Sociologists in Various Regions" *The American Sociologist*, vol. 4, no. 1, pp. 1-4.

Sykes, Charles J. 1988. *ProfScam: Professors and the Demise of Higher Education*. New York, St. Martin's Press.

Underhill, Frank H. 1960. *In Search of Canadian Liberalism*. Toronto, Macmillan.

Wells, Alan. 1979. "Conflict Theory and Functionalism: Introductory Sociology Textbooks, 1928-1976" *Teaching Sociology*, vol. 6, no. 4, pp. 429-437.

Westfall, William. 1989. *Two Worlds: The Protestant Culture of Nineteenth-Century Ontario*. Montreal, McGill-Queen's University Press.

Westhues, Kenneth. 1976. "The Adaptation of the Roman Catholic Church in Canadian Society" in S. Crysdale and L. Wheatcraft, eds., *Religion in Canadian Society*. Toronto, Macmillan.

White, Hayden. 1973. *Metahistory: The Historical Imagination in Nineteenth-Century Europe*. Baltimore, The Johns Hopkins University Press.

White, Hayden. 1978. *Tropics of Discourse: Essays in Culture Criticism*. Baltimore, John Hopkins University Press.

Wilcox-Magill, Dennis William. 1983. "Paradigms and Social Science in English Canada" in J. Paul Grayson, ed., *Introduction to Sociology: An Alternate Approach*. Toronto, Gage.

Wilson, Edward F. 1874. *Manual of the Ojebway Language*. Toronto, Society for Promoting Christian Knowledge. Reprinted in 1975 by the Department of Indian Affairs and Northern Development as The Ojebway Language.